Addict Child

A mother's journey

Lesley Sefton

For Laura and the family that love her

Dearest Addict,

Reach out to your loved ones

Explain how you love them

They are concerned for you

With every beat of your heart

CONTENTS

1. DESCENT

The telephone rang. A dreaded sound in our home. I stopped listening to the television while Rob answered. I looked at the window to my reflection. 'Where is she?' He asked. He put the phone down and turned to me, sorrow swamped his face. 'She's on a life support machine. They're not sure she'll make it through the night.'

Please God no, tell her I love her.

'Do you want to go and see her?' Rob asked.

With every nerve ready for action, I wanted to rip down the motorway to sit by her bedside and hold her hand as she passed from this life to the next. I was with her at birth; I should be beside her in death. But I could not. I was frightened by the sight of her. What she had dragged me through made this duty an unbearable task.

A brick wall had erected in my soul with stones supplied by my daughter's life. The stress I endured through Rob's cancer cemented these stones in place. I had to be strong. I had to protect my sanity, for I could not save hers. I left my daughter on a life support machine to be comforted by strangers. And my heart shattered into tiny slivers of ruby red.

The powerful allure of alcohol had beckoned my daughter; the wonder of drugs had seduced her. For twelve years I fought for her release from both. Had I ever considered my daughter might die? On several occasions, on many a day. I was resigned to the eventuality of losing her, but it is no less painful to be pragmatic. I was afraid of, and afraid for, her. The Grim Reaper lured me to draw comfort from her departure. How awful is that! To wish your baby dead.

Rob and I waited for morning, when news eventually reached us. Our daughter was out of danger, recovering in an intensive care ward. We did not visit her, we did not have the strength of mind, and Rob was gaunt and grey, his illness was apparent; our darling daughter did not know her beloved dad was seriously ill.

The days ticked into nights while our daughter regained strength, though her mind plundered into a deeper sect of darkness. She was transferred to a mental health ward. Years ago, I had begged for this to happen, and now that it had I roamed through the obscurity of sorrow. I was afraid to visit her. I was afraid to let my mind slip off that dark cliff, the one she had pulled me down so often. I could not allow shady scenarios to play in my head, to add to the ones already dredging there. My daughter would have to spend this time alone, without her family. The mere thought of this shredded my innards. Never would I have imagined staying away from my beautiful daughter while she languished in hospital. Instead, I would staple together my broken emotions, pick out the thorns that spiked me, and wait in hope that she would benefit from this incarceration.

My child was an alcoholic drug abuser, a sentence no loving parent should have to string together, though there were periods when she was sober, when she was welcomed back to our lives, and then she would just drift back out again, taking our broken hearts with her. If there was an end to this cycle of addiction, I could not see it.

With immense pain, I watched my daughter deteriorate. I hated the imposter residing in her skin. I was terrified of the stranger she had become. I was thrown into turmoil whenever the telephone rang: was it her on the other end? To demand, to beg? She put huge emotional demands on me. Demands she knew I would pass on to her dad and tether us to her determined destruction.

My alcohol-soaked daughter convinced herself we did not love her. Her perception of the world had become so different to ours. She imagined her dad, her sister and I had left her behind, that we did not want her in our lives. She was wrong. We distanced ourselves for our own protection. Her warped interpretation of love led her further into the arms of substance abuse.

How my daughter travelled this path is easy to chronicle, but why she arrived there is a mystery to me. I knew she suffered. Her desperation rocked my calm. I was a little boat riding the waves of an ocean.

There is a universal human appetite to satisfy one's needs that all addicts understand. A craving that is fed at a cost to themselves and those who love them. It is a concentrated essence of oneself. This is the hardest concept for any loved one of an addict to understand. I look back to my daughter's childhood, her rearing at my hands. Did I contribute to her downfall? I cannot find the link that led her astray. She had a happy childhood alongside her sister, Rachael. She was, and is, loved dearly.

She was born on January 18, 1977, a cold and blustery night. Ripped out of my belly by clinical hands and thrust into the world. A prolonged and difficult birth. Her struggle to life outside the womb; the harsh reality of glaring lights; the mood of the weather? Were these factors in her downfall? I am in my twelfth year of asking. There is no reason why.

You know my baby has grown to be an addict. I shall not take you through every aspect of her childhood. I suspect your interest will be in the trauma of a family coping with addiction. But I will share some key moments in her life so you might see she had a full and vital life before inviting alcohol and drugs into her world.

My daughter's name is Laura. She was a beautiful child, a special soul.

Traits of addiction

Rob and I were young parents, he was twenty-two, and I twenty-one, when Laura burst into our lives. We wanted her, we planned for her, and we adored her. No child was wanted more.

After a traumatic birthing, I lay on my back in a brightly lit side-room on the maternity unit. Rob sat in a chair by my side. A nurse dressed in navy blue came into the room, trundling a Perspex cot and woke me. I looked at the baby asleep in the cot. 'You've had a baby girl,' Rob said. I did not recognise this baby. I did not know who she was.

Three days later, I still had not recovered. A nurse stood by my bedside, cradling my baby. 'Say hi to your mummy,' the woman said, the woman who knew my baby better than me. I took a peek. I drifted back to sleep, comforted by what I understood.

My baby was content to be fed by a bottle given to her by a nurse. My inexperience did not tell me I could have taken over and breastfed Baby Laura.

The hormone oxytocin is released in large amounts during and after childbirth. It is known as the bonding hormone. Had mine depleted after a three-day separation from my baby? A bonding opportunity lost? I do not think so. I love her dearly, and she loves me.

Baby and I went home after two weeks in hospital. I was nervous of her, my new baby. She had drunk a full bottle of milk for the nurse; she would only drink half for me. But far from being a neurotic mother, I soon identified with motherhood and relaxed into the role.

Rob pulled on overalls to work long hours so I could stay home and nurture our baby daughter. We owned our own house, on a popular housing estate.

My baby did not like to be held tight, to be embraced or cuddled. I held her as if in a hammock, my arm under her back for support to keep her body away from mine. She was content with this space between us. Was this an indication of things to come, her need to be free?

Today, I look at a photograph of her as a baby. She is asleep, lying on her tummy with her bottom in the air; white frills cover her nappy. The sun pierces the room to highlight the lemon walls. This picture was snapped through the bars of her cot to capture her gentle face at peace. My baby behind bars: I did not know she would become a prisoner of addiction, no mother would.

Laura was twenty-two months old when we visited my sister's house for bonfire night. Her cousin placed a sparkler in Laura's hand. He covered her hand with his and drew her name in fizzing stars. The same cousin cried when a spark off the bonfire hit his leg. I comforted him in the kitchen. We went home. Laura held her soft baby hand out to me. A burn from the sparkler had melted a hole in her palm that needed professional attention. Yet she had not cried, had shown no pain from the burn. I thought she was brave. Should I have been concerned at this lack of physical pain?

5

Recently, I read about a condition known as congenital insensitivity to pain, and I saw no other indication in Laura to suggest she had this condition.

Laura was two years old when her sister Rachael arrived. Like Laura, Rachael was delivered by caesarean section. Unlike my first delivery, I did not feel unwell, my body now used to the trauma. I lay on my side in a darkened room. Rob sat behind me. A nurse marched into the room to check on me, and I awoke. 'You've had a little girl,' Rob said.

'Little!' the nurse interrupted. 'She's a whopper.' Rob walked around the bed to face me. He took hold of my hand and looked at me. I saw a troubled expression.

'What's wrong, is the baby okay?' I asked. 'Why are you looking at me like that?'

'Baby's fine. You've got blood splattered on your face.' I fell back to sleep. It would be the next day before I would meet my baby girl. She was wheeled into the room in a similar Perspex cot her sister had slept in. I looked in and recognised her instantly, her pretty face a reflection of Laura's. I held Rachael, I breastfed her, it was a beautiful, sunny September day. In those days, children were not allowed to visit the maternity unit for fear of infection. I was parted from my toddler Laura during my confinement. I had left my child at home, the child I doted on. After two weeks, I came home to Laura with happiness wrapped in a blanket. My toddler's mind was unfurling; could she imagine she had been replaced? A child does not comprehend a mother's love is boundless and can encompass all her babies. Did Laura feel rejected? I do not know. We lived in the times we lived in, we followed the rules of the day. Professionals at the hospital considered the risk of infection, but they spared no thought to the risk of affection.

Laura was a demanding child. She was our child, and we loved her. She gave us warmth, she gave us fun. A determined individual who had a tantrum one day at two-and-a-half years old. I took her by the hand and marched her to her bedroom. I plonked her on the floor. 'Stop screaming!' I demanded. I left her on the floor and closed the bedroom door. She howled louder. I entered her room to explain, and she understood, that if she stopped misbehaving she could come downstairs. Her pitch climbed to a higher note. She shrieked to exhaustion and fell asleep on the floor before she would give in to me.

Laura needed to be entertained, she would follow me around the house, copying the jobs I did. I cleaned the windows one day. From the top of the stepladder, I looked down to see her rubbing the window in the same manner. 'Where have you got that dirty rag from?' I asked.

'Marks and Spencer,' replied my three-year-old.

Her idea of playing with a Barbie doll was to chop its hair off and discard it. She did not construct imaginary games, she preferred to go to the park or visit friends. She enjoyed socialising. Ironic that as an adult she forced seclusion on herself.

Laura was a deep thinker, she amused us all with her take on life. 'How long would it take to parachute from the moon?' She enquired, looking into the night sky. I drove my car to the town, my two girls strapped in the back. Laura sparked up: 'Do gums have freckles?' 'Do false teeth need fillings?'

In the bathroom sat Laura's new toothbrush, the bristles splayed from brushing too hard. 'You're not having spends this week. They're going to another toothbrush. Why do you always have to learn the hard way? Why do you always swim upstream?'

Sorting laundry into piles, I found Laura's knickers were ripped at the seam. 'Laura,' I shouted. I waited for her to walk into the room. I held up several pairs of her knickers. 'Why are these ripped?'

'I don't like the feel of them on my skin.'

'For goodness' sake, child, what will you come up with next?'

There is a knicker tale of which I am ashamed. Laura, immersed in pool water, awaited instruction from the swimming teacher. Laura's right hand fiddled with the bottom of her swimming costume. The other five children kicked off from the side of the pool and began swimming. Laura swam with one hand while pulling her costume out of her bottom with the other. I hung over the balcony and shouted down to her. At the end of the lesson I waited on the sideline with a fluffy towel to wrap her in. 'Why were you messing about with your costume when you should have been concentrating on swimming?' I rubbed the towel to keep her warm.

'I could feel my costume on my skin.'

In the changing room, I helped her dress. I withheld her knickers.

'You won't be needing these, as you don't like the feel of them.' Outside, with no underwear on, the wind whipped up her dress. Her friend saw Laura's peach of a bottom and reported it to school the next day. I often wonder if my parenting style was too harsh. Had Laura been granted the wrong family?

About this time, story read and tucked into bed, Laura should have been asleep. I had kissed her two hours earlier. She stood at the top of the stairs and called my name. I went to the hall and up the stairs to her. 'I sucked a lead pencil today,' she said. 'Will I die?'

'No, course not, don't be silly. But don't do it again.' I re-tucked her into bed and kissed her forehead. I loved my funny, uptight little girl. Around this time, when Laura was six, I waited for her outside the school gates. Usually the last one out, today she was first. She refused to hold my hand. She walked home with concern on her face. I asked, 'What's up?'

'I was sitting on the stage; when I got up I fell over and touched Flora's head. Everyone says she's got nits. Look at my hand. It's got white spots on it.' I took her hand and rubbed warmth into it.

'Circulation spots, not nits. You are a silly girl.'

At eight years old, Laura was to be a bridesmaid to her aunty. Her pretty peach dress hung on the door, along with Rachael's. There was excitement in the house. I kissed both girls, bedded down in their separate rooms. 'Sleep now, big day tomorrow,' I said to each daughter. An hour passed.

We heard Laura cry out. Rob and I rushed upstairs and found Laura sitting straight up in bed. 'I don't know where I am,' she said.

'What do you mean?' I asked. Fear creeping into my belly.

'Get to sleep,' Rob demanded. He closed the door.

'Do you think she's all right?'

'Of course, she is. Don't go looking for things that aren't there.'

9

Little seeds of doubt over my daughter's wellbeing were sewn into my gut. Little seeds of doubt I did not know what to do with. Should I water them or dig them out? Were these feelings of uncertainty traits of addiction? How would I know? I was a young mother with two children to raise. My time, my thoughts, my energy, were swallowed by the task.

As a family we travelled for leisure, and relaxed in sunny climates abroad. We sunbathed by a swimming pool, we swam in the sea. We climbed mountains and swallowed the shallow air. We ingested culture from Egypt and visited a bazaar where jasmine incense infused the air. We listened to the haunting call for prayer, echoing in the night air. We rode around the pyramids on horseback. We shuffled around the museum that held King Tut's artefacts, glad to be away from the sun's boundless energy. Back on the street, we saw the stagnant traffic and heard the constant bleating of horns attempting to force drivers along. The dust in the air darkened our skin. In America, we hired a car and drove to the amusement parks. Our laughter combined as our bodies left the seat of a ride. We drove down the Florida coastline and vacationed on the Keys. My girls played with a racoon until an American lady flung the hotel window open and shouted, 'Get those children away! Racoons carry rabies!' We witnessed incredible sunsets at Key West, the huge sun sinking into the sea, burning bright red with warmth. At home, we took picnics to the seaside and played commandos in the sand dunes. Before driving home, we had a game of rounders on the beach. We walked in step on the untrodden ground of the countryside that surrounded our home. We dined in restaurants. Our eyes danced to the tune of conversation, our appetites warmed to the aroma of garlic. Laura enjoyed those times; we all did.

In her eighth year, Laura was awarded swimming medals: bronze, silver, and gold. A written piece in the newspaper published her achievement. Laura was fearless of water, sea, or pool: she never considered what lurked beneath. She joined the Brownie Brigade and progressed to Girl Guides. She learnt to play the piano, but did not enjoy the practice and stopped attending lessons.

Two years later, we moved to a bigger house, brand new and still on a building site. Laura would dig for treasure in the excavation piles of unearthed soil. Rachael and their cousins joined in the search. From these finds, Laura collected antique bottles, mostly chipped, muddy and dull but sparkling after she cleaned them: white bottles, green bottles, and some that were blue. I did not know empty bottles would feature in her adult life.

When Laura was twelve, she had braces fitted to her teeth because some teeth were missing and would never grow. Was something lacking in her genes? She had tooth formation, delayed or absent. Corrective treatment would minimise the fault in her teeth, and braces would pull the front teeth together. When maturity was reached, Laura had bridge work done to both sides of the rear of her mouth. We travelled back and forth to the orthodontist in the city, the city where she now lives. I prefer she lives in the city. I prefer she lives away from me. Harrowing to bump into her in the town, to see her face, to see she has been drinking again.

So, we have a teenager, a cuckoo in our nest. Laura's early teens were spent in our company, with the family she loved. We continued to do what we enjoyed. Was she a moody teenager? At times, like all teenagers. She left no footprint of what lay ahead.

Accomplished liar

Sweet sixteen, we held a party for Laura in a pub. To be ready for her party she went to the hairdresser for a permanent head of curls. 'Perms are very hit and miss,' I warned.

'I'm having it done.' Forced curls in the hair were the fashion of the day, and Laura wanted to follow the trend. She had started to ignore my input, she had started to feel her own way. She cried on arriving home from the hairdresser, having taken a lonely route to avoid being seen. I heard her key in the lock, and through the door she came. She paused at the hall mirror to check if the horrendous style was true. I stood behind her.

'Looks like pubes all over my head,' she said.

A laugh escaped me. 'I'll cut it in layers to take the volume out,' I offered. I lifted clumps of hair as she watched through the reflection of the mirror.

'Can you do that? Won't it make it worse?'

'Nah, how can you make that worse?' Oh, how I wished I had left her hair alone. I cut, then hacked, at the wayward perm. The hair would not be tamed, it was outrageously independent. The coiled curls sprang from every direction, I could not coax them flat. I devised a style to tame the unruly locks: a French plait up the back of her head to pull in the strands. I clipped the hair on top of her head with a pineapple flourish. 'There,' I said.

Laura returned to the mirror. 'It looks like a scorpion on my head.' She thundered to her room to dry her tears and get ready for her party.

We travelled to the party in silence. Popular scent perfumed the car. Rachael sat by Laura's side on the back seat of the car. Glancing sideways at her sister's hairstyle, Rachael kept her mouth shut. At the venue, Rob and I waited at the bar. Our girls went up the stairs to join their friends in the party room. The teenagers danced to music, ordered soft-drinks, and later, I discovered, drank smuggled alcohol. The door upstairs opened. 'Rhythm is a Dancer' by Snap escaped the room. Laura with a friend exited to the beat of the tune. They walked past Rob and me. Ignoring our presence, they headed for the toilet. My heart went out to Laura. She was dressed in a pair of patterned trousers, a white blouse, and black waistcoat, bang on trend, but the hair? There was nothing remotely fashionable there.

Laura wore this hairstyle for six months, the only choice she had. The layers of hair grew to obedience, and it was time for a haircut at a decent hairdresser. The snip of sharp scissors slid across her hair with precision and created a bob style at jaw level. The style suited her. She looked beautiful, stunning. Her time had come to bloom.

We were a family unit still, spending leisure time and holidays together.

Laura had a girl-like plumpness, in no way fat to a mother's eye. Super skinny was the fashion of the day, and Laura wanted to comply. She stood next to me when I prepared meals to direct every serving. 'Don't put much on my plate, and I don't want any of that.' She would point to the main ingredient.

I treated her like a child. I piled her plate high, and told her to 'get it eaten'.

She gobbled a vanilla slice one day. It disappeared in a second. Alert to this contradiction of eating pattern, I became suspicious. Minutes after her departure, I tiptoed upstairs. Traces of the custard delicacy blasted the toilet bowl. I charged to her room, my rubber gloves still on. 'Have you made yourself sick?' I demanded.

'No, why?'

'I'm not saying how I know, but I know you have.'

13

'Yes, I did. Just this once, but I won't do it again.' The first promise of many she would squeeze in her hand and break into fragments of truth. I saw no further trace of food abuse. Bulimia nervosa did not affect me, did not cause me pain. Foolishly, I ignored the possibility that my daughter had an eating disorder. For I know now that young women with bulimia are at a greater risk of substance abuse. Substances commonly abused by this population include alcohol, street drugs (cocaine and marijuana), prescribed medications, and non-psychoactive substances (laxatives, emetics, diuretics and diet pills).

Aware that my daughter had forced herself to be sick, I compromised and prepared salads with added protein. She did not become stick thin, she did not look gaunt. My daughter prepared for deception, she was proving to be an expert. Laura assured us regurgitating food was no longer a problem. I witnessed her greedy episodes, but I did not see an obsession creep into my daughter's head and find a home there.

The kissing disease

Our family unit was changing; we took our last holiday together. Laura was seventeen. All dressed for home, she knocked a glass of Coca-Cola over her dad. He was drenched by the sticky black fluid. The stress of travel and of returning to work had primed his fuse and he blew: 'Bloody hell Laura, watch what you're doing, you clumsy idiot!' He picked a serviette off the table and dabbed his clothes.

Laura responded, glaring at him. 'If you think I'm coming on holiday with you again, you can forget it.'

'That's something you've got right.' Rob frowned at her. He slapped the wet serviette on the table.

That summer, Laura took a holiday with friends at a caravan park not far from home. The girls returned with dirty clothes, and boyfriends. These courtships lasted in written form for a few months. I searched out one of the love letters addressed to my daughter, then wished I had not. Crude drawings of sex acts had been sent to her. I folded the offensive letter, shoved it back in the envelope, and washed my hands. I was glad when that friendship fizzled out. I hoped Laura felt the same way as me: disgusted.

Laura's hair is dark, jet, her eyes are brilliant blue. She has a quality, a look, you would describe as striking, unique. And so she found makeup and lots of it. She worked like an artist on her eyes to perfect a glamorous look, her way not mine. I spoilt her with fashion; we shopped for the latest designs.

Laura caught the attention of the popular boy at school and he took her out on a date. She had tasted admiration and wanted more. Sadly, the boy died at the tender age of eighteen. He would never reach manhood, he would never sow his seed. By dangerous driving, he took his own life. His funeral was Laura's first. She cried for days.

When Laura was eighteen, she arranged travel to sun-soaked Tenerife. No coincidence she and her friends chose the date to embrace exam results day. She signed to have her A-level results posted.

Six months earlier, I had 'found' a report from college. This would be my last root in her drawer for the trouble it caused: the report was dire. Laura returned home from college. I was desperate to challenge her on my find. First, I gave her the chance to confess. 'Have you been given a report from college?' I asked.

'No, it's only the failing students who get reports.'

Unbelievable! I asked her to bring in the washing, and then I ran upstairs for the report.

Laura returned to the kitchen, a laundry basket of damp clothes in her hands. I held out the yellow form.

'Oh,' she said. Then pleaded with me not to tell her dad.

'No, but you can.' She chose not to, and went out of the back door while Rob and I sat out front. She disappeared down the street. She gave me no choice. My held breath escaped, and I told him.

'She can come out of that college. She's taking the piss. Does she think she's on a two-year coffee break? She can leave and get a full-time job.' He slammed his cup of half-drunk coffee on the floor. 'She's a bloody waste of space.' He went inside. His wishes were made known to Laura when she returned home. She screwed her mouth tight and shook her head at me.

At Rob's request, I drove Laura to the local factory to enquire if there was a vacancy to train as a machinist, stitching knickers for Marks and Spencer. I waited in the car, she walked the factory floor alone to taste the clatter of machines, feel the heat from the steam press, and listen to the idle chatter. She climbed into the car, an application form in her hand. 'Please, Mum, I want to stay at college. Please don't make me work there. I promise to knuckle down and study. Please, Mum.'

'You need to speak with Dad. This is up to him.' I begged Rob to let Laura stay at college. He agreed, for he would do anything to please me.

Laura telephoned from her holiday in Tenerife, an incident to report. 'Mum, there was an intruder in our room, rifling through our belongings. I got out of bed and punched her.'

'Bloody hell, Laura.' I gripped the telephone tighter.

'I had to go to the police station to make a statement and look at pictures of offenders.'

'Why is it always you?'

'What have I done wrong?'

I sighed deep enough to feel the vibration through the telephone line. No charge was made against the intruder, no charge was made against my daughter. I used to think Laura was unlucky and drew bad karma her way. Today, I know different. She shaped misfortune with her own fair hands. Evening approached night. The telephone rang, again from Tenerife. 'Mum, we've been kicked out of our apartment.'

'Kicked out, why?'

'Because we wouldn't let the maid in. We were sleeping when she came round. They say we have to pay for screwed up sheets.'

'Seriously?'

'Anyway, we're waiting for our rep. She'll find alternative accommodation for us to stay.'

'So why are you telling me? There's nothing I can do.'

'Just thought you'd want to know.' The telephone line clicked, dead. The first experience of being helpless on the end of a telephone line, of worrying into the night because of a conversation between my daughter and me.

The envelope that shielded Laura's exam results had landed. She had requested that I not open it. She did not want me to relay the results over the telephone and interfere with her holiday pleasure. I collected Laura from the airport. In the car, I asked about her holiday. I quizzed her about her expectation of exam results. She shrugged. She was tired from travelling and two weeks of partying. I missed the junction I should have taken off the motorway, my concentration focused on prising information from her. We headed in a direction I did not understand. 'Bloody hell,' I said, 'I don't know my way home from here.'

'For God's sake, Mum, I can do without this.'

'You can do without this? I don't know where we're going.' I have an irrational fear of getting lost, of falling off the face of the earth. A sensible person would have found the next exit to rejoin the motorway in the opposite direction. Leave at the next roundabout, and gain access to the motorway travelling in the right direction, then exit at the correct junction. My phobia would not allow this thought process to flow. We travelled along the road in silence.

'I recognise this area,' Laura said. Where she knew it from, I did not ask. I was grateful for direction, and we resumed the path home.

I opened the front door. Tanned, slim and beautiful, Laura dragged her suitcase into the hall. The exam envelope sat in the middle of the worktop in the kitchen. She walked past the brown envelope and gave it a sideways glance. I picked it up and held it out to her: 'Open it.'

'Give me a chance.' She snatched the envelope from my hand and tore open the seal. All subjects failed. Oh, and her best subject, the one she said she was really good at: marked unclassified. For two years' support: nothing! I took a ragged breath. Without a word, Laura went to her room and flopped on her bed. Concern bubbled in me as I waited for Rob to return home and tell him the news, how our daughter had wasted her opportunity at college.

'What did I tell you? Should have taken her out of college months ago,' he said. There was nothing I could add to his comment. I had wanted to believe in our daughter, Rob did not. I wanted Laura to make something of her life, gain a career. Rob wanted his daughter to get a job, any job. Support herself as an adult, not the child I allowed her to be.

Rob thought this to be hilarious: the college sent a letter inviting Laura to enrol for A-level resit. 'No,' he said. 'She can get a job.'

Laura had a part-time job selling pasties at a well-known bakery, in a uniform she detested. She asked for, and was granted, extra hours. But it was a job, not a career. I would not give up on her future prospects. I scanned the local newspapers. I saw an advert: a two-year course to train as a dental nurse practitioner, with a small bursary included. Laura and I sat in the back garden to fill out the application form. 'Go and post it,' I said.

'I'll do it later.'

'Go and post it.' I watched her walk down the drive, the white envelope in her hand. The following week, she applied for an administration post in the civil service. As a result, Laura was invited to interview for the two positions, she was accepted for both. She chose the dental hospital in the city. We were off and running.

She went on the train to the city and made new friends at the dental hospital. She took a holiday in Cyprus with this bunch of girls. She came home suntanned and relaxed. I scrutinised her holiday snaps looking for cigarettes in ashtrays. I paired the sticks of nicotine to each girl in the photo. My daughter matched one. Her eyes looked wasted, her face shone happiness. Bless her, I thought. Don't all teenagers drink alcohol on holiday? One week later, Laura was ill with glandular fever: the kissing disease. Laura's attendance at the dental course halted. One night during her illness she hallucinated. I got into bed with her and held her. I spent the night by her side and waited for her fever to abate. Laura spent weeks at home recovering. She wanted to get on with her course, to get on with her life.

Laura returned to the dental hospital and caught up with her studies. She returned to socialising.

A mother's mission

Time for Laura to learn how to drive a car. I took her out in my car to supplement her paid lessons. She drove the car around a corner with her foot pressed down on the clutch pedal. 'Don't do that,' I instructed. 'You're free-wheeling.' She straightened the car and continued down the road.

'What was I doing? Driving on three wheels.' We shared many a laugh with Laura, her time with us was not all heartache.

Laura failed the driving test at the first attempt. She sat in the car with the examiner, placed her left hand on the handbrake, juggled her feet to biting point, looked in the rear-view mirror, in the side mirror, and over her right shoulder for the blind spot. Off with the handbrake, up with her left foot, down with her right: nothing. 'I think you should turn the key in the ignition,' the examiner prompted. It took four attempts for Laura to pass the driving test. Rob and I bought her a car, a VW hatchback, brushed gold, one lady owner, low mileage – his choice not hers.

During this time, I answered the telephone. 'I've run out of petrol,' Laura said. I turned the oven off, closed the windows, and took the petrol can out of the garage. I headed to the petrol station and filled the container with fuel. I drove to where Laura was stranded.

'For goodness sake, Laura!'

'I didn't know it was empty.'

'Look next time. I'm not doing this again.' In times to come, I would have given anything for my mission of mercy to be so simple.

One evening, Laura drove around the town with friends in her car. Somehow she had left the tailgate open. The car stereo boomed the latest dance tune into the night air: a mobile disco. She drove around the town with the tailgate bouncing. People waved, trying to alert her to the open door. Oblivious, she returned each wave. She told this tale to Rob and me in hilarious detail.

Later that year, 'I've had a bump in my car,' Laura said, over the phone. It was late evening, Rob was out playing squash, de-stressing after work. I drove to Laura, wanting to rescue her. I waited my turn to pass through the temporary traffic lights. The feathery note in Laura's voice had assured me not to panic. I took the car's handbrake off, moved a short distance, and stopped again. I was nearing the front of the queue. I could see police cars and an ambulance. Then I drove past Laura's car and saw its back end was destroyed, smashed to smithereens. I drove with speed to the nearest side street and abandoned my car. I ran to Laura, my breath short, my chest tight. In the distance, Laura stood on the footpath to the side of the carnage, professionals swarmed the scene. Thankfully, there was not a mark on her, she was unhurt. Laura was faultless in the collision. A young lad had rear-ended her car. Travelling at considerable speed, he was distracted by the task of changing the music on his music player and was unprepared for the temporary lights, the stopped cars that met him as he took a bend in the road, and smashed straight into Laura's car. Luck had wrapped herself in a cloak of bad to choose my daughter. A policeman asked Laura if she had been drinking. 'Yes, coffee,' she said. A breathalyser kit produced a negative reading. This would not be an isolated test. She did not want to get into the waiting ambulance. Instead, I took her to the hospital for a check-up. 'Good job I had taken my friends home; two of them were sitting in the back,' Laura said. I shook my head and shuddered. Laura had no major injuries, though she would suffer from whiplash come the morning. With a stiff white collar fastened around her neck, we headed home. Rob was unaware of the accident. He was still part of a team playing squash. I saw no reason to shatter his freedom.

The next day we went as a family to inspect the car at the garage it had been hauled to. We stared at the mangled wreckage. Tears pricked my eyes. I swallowed, tried to clear the tension in my throat. The car could have taken my daughter with it. I put my arm around her and rubbed her arm. We shared the same short smile.

The car was a write-off. Rob and I bought Laura a new car, a shiny red Volkswagen Polo. She preferred this one.

Cigarettes, a minor thing?

My baby, the one I had nurtured, the one I had fed milk and honey too, was filling her healthy lungs with treacle nicotine. I was not happy. Laura was smoking cigarettes.

Rob and I held an open-door policy for Laura's friends. They flocked to our house before a night out, to share cocktails, to share wine. Friends would come home with Laura to stay the night. I encouraged this. Bring my baby home safe, don't let her wander the streets at night alone. Was I over protective? Yes, I was. But Laura was my precious cargo stepping out into the greedy hands of the night.

I walked past the hall window on one such evening. Laura sat in her car, on the drive, with a friend. They were smoking cigarettes. When the girls re-entered the house, they filled the hall with the rank smell of fresh smoke. I could not contain my fury. 'What the hell do you think you're doing, smoking?' I directed my tirade at Laura and ignored her friend. Laura shot me a look of defiance. The mouth she happily opened for nicotine was tightly clamped now. Both girls went upstairs to Laura's room. Her door slammed shut. Ten minutes passed. The girls left the house without shouting goodbye. I jumped out of my seat. Rob cast me a glance. I rummaged through magazines and ripped out pictures of diseased lungs, blackened teeth, health warnings connected to tobacco. I stuck the images onto Laura's dressing table mirror. I returned to my seat, my breathing laboured.

'What've you been doing?' Rob asked. I told him.

'What's the point?'

'I want her to realise the harm she's doing.'

Rob shook his head. 'Leave her to it. You're wasting your time.'

The next morning, Laura ripped the collage of cigarette horror from her mirror. She screwed the images into a ball and chucked them in the wastebasket. 'Stay out of my room,' was all she said.

'You do know there are a lot of calories in cigarettes?' I shouted through the closed door, trying to hone in on her weight issues.

Years later, she would walk five steps behind me to spark up a fag, a roll-up at that.

So, Rob and I opened our home to a stream of teenagers. The format for weekends: girls brought alcohol, listened to music, chatted. They checked their appearances in the mirror and applied lip gloss to their lip-sticky lips before stepping out into the night.

One summer evening, two friends arrived, minus several that alcohol had been purchased for. Upstairs they trotted. Evening trickled into night, and the girls were still in residence. Rob and I wanted our bed. He shouted up the stairs, 'Time you went out.'

With giggles, and flushes of the toilet, the three of them came down the stairs each in high heels. They shouted their goodbyes as they passed through the front door.

I went to close the windows, left open for the balmy evening, and heard a commotion from the street. 'Go and have a look,' I said to Rob. 'What if the girls have bumped into thugs?' Off Rob marched in his shorts and slippers as I watched from the window. He stood at the bottom of the drive, his hands slid into his pockets. I left the house to join him. Dusk did not rob my vision of the street; I could see the commotion across the road. Laura and her two friends waited for a non-existent bus. All three girls were paralytic. I shouted my daughter's name.

'What?' she shouted back. I shouted her name again. I applied my sternest look, one she knew to respect. I folded my arms to enhance my request. Laura sauntered over to Rob and me, she took a deep pull on a cigarette, it glowed, like a ruby with flaws.

'Put that cigarette out,' I spat, dodging the smoke blown at me.

'For God's sake, I'm nineteen. You can't treat me like this.'

Rob remained silent, with a wave of annoyance building in his eyes.

'Put that cigarette out.' My teeth let the words escape. She threw the cigarette to the ground and stamped on it. 'Get inside,' I commanded.

'No, I'm going with my friends.' One friend leant over a hedge to be sick. The other peered through squinting eyes, as she struggled to focus on what was happening on our side of the street.

'Let her go. She's not worth the hassle,' Rob said. He gave his daughter a look of disdain and walked up the drive to the wide open front door.

'No, you are not going out in this state. Get inside.' Laura knew the jig was up. Even in her inebriated condition, she knew I was serious. Bemused, her friends staggered off. Laura stormed, as best she could, through the front door and into the hall.

'You should have let her go. She's a bloody disgrace,' Rob said. He could be vicious with his tongue, using words to cut people, but he never physically hurt any of us.

Laura looked directly into her dad's eyes. 'Go on then, hit me,' she taunted.

'Get out of my sight,' he said, and moved away from her.

Laura tried to goad him into an argument. She desired eruption to bubble and flow. She wanted insults to run her way. She longed to be a victim, to gain our sympathy and an apology that would allow her to leave the house to join her friends. I would not let this happen. I guided her up the stairs to her bedroom. She fell asleep on top of the covers, still wearing her mini-dress and high-heels.

Morning arrived, bringing sunshine with birdsong. Laura came into the kitchen. 'I'm sorry Mum. I'm so ashamed.' She was dressed from the night before.

Did Laura binge-drink alcohol often? Yes, she did. Her alcohol consumption was confined to Friday and Saturday nights and the odd bank holiday. Did I think this a problem? No, I did not. Her peers did the same. Laura got up in the mornings and went about her day. Was I happy with the alcohol she consumed? I positively was not. If I intervened, my daughter and I would have massive arguments. She attended her course at the dental hospital, she partied at weekends, we left it at that.

At the beginning of her studies, Laura arrived home from the dental hospital in the city. She took her coat off. I handed her a mug of steaming coffee. She tipped half the liquid down the sink and replaced the volume with milk.

'You can make your own coffee in future,' I said.

'Mum, I was so embarrassed today. This poor man lay back in the dentist chair, staring into the bright light. The dentist took the man's false teeth out causing the man's face to collapse.'

'Why would that embarrass you?'

'I fainted.'

'Laura!'

'It unnerved me seeing someone's face cave in.'

'What did the dentist say?'

'Nothing, but when the patient left, everyone started laughing.'

'What about the poor man?'

'He looked bewildered.'

Laura amazed Rob and me with her retention of knowledge: clinical names she knew, and what they meant.

She thrived on the dental course. Exams passed, Laura became a registered dental nurse. I sat in the audience with a broad smile on my face, watching the dental nurses step up on stage, one by one, to receive their certificates.

Laura applied for and acquired a post as a district dental nurse, visiting local schools. Before taking the position, she was asked to remain and work at the hospital where she had trained. She chose the hospital. She stuck to what she knew.

Laura had money to spend, and spend it she did.

After six months employment, the dental hospital was forced to make cutbacks, and Laura was looking for a job. A local dentist advertised a nurse position and Laura went to the interview in the evening. She sat in a room full of hopefuls, but none had her qualification. Before she arrived home from the interview I took a message. The job was hers. She was pleased, and so were we.

A shift pattern at the dental practice meant no two weeks were the same. Scrutiny of the payslip showed Laura had taken a part-time job. She had understood at the interview that there would be extra hours of work if needed. A misunderstanding: their need to be met, not hers. I understood reduced contractual hours equated to reduced benefits. Still, Laura was happy, and the months ticked by. She had reached her twenty-first birthday. Laura celebrated this milestone with friends at a popular Italian restaurant. Rob popped into the venue before the party, ordered wine to flow at his expense. For extended family, we threw a house party. Laura chose a few friends to join in. I put the record on we bought for her birth: a cover version of Stevie Wonder's Isn't She Lovely by David Parton. I gave a speech. 'Happy birthday Laura, how lucky for you to have both sets of grandparents at your twenty-first.' She was mortified. I filmed the event. Each time the camera pointed her way, she turned away to share her annoyance with friends. I had become an embarrassment to her.

No abuse of alcohol at this party. Laura behaved in the company of relatives, for now.

Ghost of a wedding

Ten months after her twenty-first birthday, Laura brought home a young man to meet us. The man was tall, dark, and mm … okay, handsome. He crept into my daughter's heart and burrowed there for three years. He proposed marriage then scurried away, leaving a scar in his absence. John was a drip of a lad who should have married his mother and left my daughter alone. Saved us from all the time and expense.

During early courtship, Laura suffered recurring tonsillitis. Like a bad boyfriend, the tonsils needed whipping out. I will tell you this about my daughter, she is brave. Not a problem for her to have an operation, not a problem for her to be in pain. Laura's frustration lay in the recovery period. She wanted to feel better instantly. 'I love the experience of the anaesthetic,' she said. 'I love to float away.' I should have been alarmed.

I spoke my own thoughts on anaesthesia. 'No, I hate it, I worry I won't wake again.' See how different we are, my daughter and I. John did not visit Laura in hospital, nor visit her sickbed at home. Said he might faint. He sent flowers instead.

Laura's job at the dental practice paid two weeks sick-leave per year. The low benefits of this job had started to show. It was time for Laura to move on, and I made a suggestion: 'I've spoken with Dad. Why don't you apply to train as a nurse? We'll support you until you qualify.' Three years support to qualify as a Registered General Nurse. Laura embraced the offer, she grasped it with both hands. After

28

attending an interview, she was accepted at the university hospital. She was back on the train to the city.

'I know this train journey like the back of my head,' she said. We laughed.

Laura acquired a new clutch of friends, easy for her, being gregarious and likeable. The nurse training was split into blocks. Weeks on campus, weeks on a hospital ward. Laura returned home after her first day on a ward and sat crying on the stairs. 'It was awful today. I helped to lay out an old lady. She had such a peaceful look on her face.' Laura blew her nose. I squeezed in next to her on the stairs to stroke her back. 'I was asked to open the window to let her spirit fly out. Then we took her to Rose Cottage.'

'Rose Cottage?'

'It's what they call the mortuary.' New phrases Laura was learning, new phrases she passed onto me. I pulled a strand of hair from her face and fixed it in the band holding her ponytail. Her first day on a hospital ward had been overwhelming, but like all first days never to be forgotten, the day blended into the rest of the working week as a month flew by.

Laura flourished on this course. She loved all aspects of nursing, especially nursing the elderly; she had an affinity with them. One elderly lady asked Laura to meet her friends. Laura followed her patient to a mirror. 'Look,' the lady said, pointing at their reflections. 'There they are, in there.'

Laura joined a nursing bank, working extra hours at different locations, both for money and experience.

One Easter: Laura was out with friends enjoying a night on the town. John was out with his mates doing the same. With a drink in her hand, Laura surveyed the dance floor. She spotted John, and he acknowledged her. She turned to tell her friend that she would go over to him. Laura downed her drink, looked to her destination. John had gone. A tug on Laura's arm, she swirled around, a smile on her face. Not John, but a man had demanded Laura's attention, a man she did not know. 'Are you going out with John?' the messenger asked.

'Yes, we've been together for six months.' Laura thought he had picked up on John's ignorance.

'Oh,' said the stranger. 'You know there's a girl pregnant with his baby?' Laura scanned the dance floor, searched for John to rubbish this information. He had disappeared when the secret flew out of the bottle.

Laura carried an emptiness inside her belly and rocked the night away at her friend's house. Night chased day. Laura returned home in the morning. She recounted the baby tale to Rob and me.

'Get rid of him.' Was my advice.

'Hang on.' Rob jumped in. 'Let the lad have his say.'

'It's the deceit I couldn't live with,' I said. Laura shrugged her shoulders. She took her bag to her room.

Laura summoned John and he appeared in the afternoon. 'We're going for a walk,' she said. John's mouth did not open, and his eyes scanned the floor. I knew the baby tale to be true.

Laura came back from the walk alone. She shared this time-honoured fable: 'It was a one-night stand before we met. He was drunk at a party. Doesn't even know whether the baby is his.'

'Why didn't he tell you this when you first got together? And why did he run away from you last night?' I asked. Rob listened.

'Said he felt bad about that. The guilt of all this weighed heavy on him. Said he felt like shit last week when we all went out for that meal.'

'Oh, poor him,' I said. 'Didn't spoil his appetite.' Rob shot me a look. 'So, what are you going to do?'

Laura shrugged her shoulders for a second time. I knew she had made her up mind. Forgive him, is what she would do.

'All I know,' Rob added, 'is you seem very happy together.' They were always giggling.

'I know, and it happened before he went out with me.' Laura favoured Dad's comment, as I walked away to put the kettle on for a cup of tea to cleanse my sorrow.

I told Rachael the delicate news. Rachael was dismayed but accepted her sister's decision as right for her.

Not long after this news, we were all invited to a family celebration: my nephew's eighteenth birthday party. Laura stayed home, ill with a bladder infection. John was too busy to visit Laura on her sickbed. I came home early from the party with a carton of cranberry juice. I entered the house. Upstairs, Laura was on the telephone, crying. I tiptoed to the bottom of the stairs to hear her plead. 'Please don't finish with me. I do forgive you for the baby thing. I promise I won't mention it again. No, no I won't, please.'

Hold me back! I slammed on my brakes. My beautiful, unique daughter deserved better than this. She had done no wrong. John held his and Laura's future together in his dirty, clumsy hands. The telephone clicked, the air was silent. I scooted away from the bottom of the stairs before Laura descended. Instead of her usual thunderous gait, she walked softly down the stairs. She wiped her nose on a sodden tissue.

'What are you doing home?' she asked.

'I came home to be with you. Everything all right?'

'Yes, why wouldn't it be?'

'Oh, no reason,' I could not admit to my eavesdropping. 'How are you feeling?'

'Lousy.'

Laura masked her feelings of betrayal. She obeyed John: the baby issue no longer a problem she could air.

To inflate her earnings, Laura took a Saturday job at a department store where she sprayed particles of perfume at passersby. Time shared with John amounted to three evenings a week.

The mystery baby was born: a girl. The mother named the baby Helena. Laura's demeanour sank. 'We'd talked about names for a baby. Helena was the name we chose for when we have a baby of our own.' I had no comment for that. John carried this baby's picture in his wallet. A picture of a baby he reckoned was not his. He made plans to visit the newborn.

'You should go with him,' I said. 'If the child is his, then she's going to be part of both your lives.'

Laura agreed.

My daughter obliged his instruction. She waited outside in the car while John disappeared into the baby-mother's house to see, what he pretended, was another man's offspring.

Time moved on. Laura settled with John. Two years of the three-year nursing course had been completed. Rob and I arrived home from a holiday. Laura rushed to greet us. 'Guess what?' she said. 'I've got engaged.' I walked to the sitting room and sat on the settee. Laura plonked down next to me.

'Engaged? But you haven't finished the nursing course,' I said. 'You're still a student.'

'I know. But he asked me, and I said yes.'

Laura threw out her left hand to show the engagement ring. She allowed the stone to sparkle.

Rob and I peered at her hand. 'That's lovely,' I said. 'Where did you choose it from?'

'I didn't. It was a surprise.'

'That is romantic.' I warmed to my daughter being engaged.

'He took his mother with him; she chose the ring.' Words I had I left unsaid. Rob kissed the top of Laura's head, then left the room. I cried.

'What's up, Mum?'

'Nothing,' I lied. 'I'm just happy for you.'

John came to visit. Rob opened a bottle of champagne. We chinked glasses high in the air to wish them both well.

Secretly over the years, Rob and I had scraped together a considerable nest egg for Laura's future. The country was in the clutches of a house-buying boom, and prices were rising fast. If we declared the savings we had for her, she would be able to surf the tide of soaring prices. We confided in her about the lump sum coming her way, strictly for the deposit on a house. 'Really?' she said.

'Really,' we replied. Proud smiles stretched across Rob's face and mine. Laura left the room to telephone John. I scanned the local newspaper for a house to buy. Laura returned and sat by my side to view the open page of house sales. 'What did John say?' I asked.

'He's shocked. He can't believe it either.'

Laura and John scouted the estate agents. They found a house they liked, a semi-detached house on a tree-lined street, with cut-glass windows and a pretty garden. Rob and I took a trip to see the house and we agreed, it was perfect. The pre-newlyweds made an offer on the house and it was accepted. John's parents inspected the house. They wanted to see it through their eyes, imagine their son living there. Laura returned home from this visit alone. 'We're not buying that house,' she said.

'What? I thought you loved that house,' I said. I wrapped both hands around the garden rake I was using. I could not believe what I was hearing.

'We do, but his mum doesn't like it.'

'It's your choice, yours and John's,' Rob said. He put the watering can down to look at his daughter.

Laura engaged with her dad's eyes. 'That's what I said, but he won't budge. If his mother says no, well that's that.' Rob and I had nothing to say. Laura went inside the house, unsurprised by our shocked silence.

I looked at Rob, my eyebrows raised. 'What do you think of that?'

'Ridiculous! What sort of man is he?' Rob walked over to the tap on the outside wall and refilled the watering can. I followed him.

'I told you she should have sacked him after that baby business,' I spat. Rob did not respond.

The pre-marital couple drove around areas they would like to live in and found another house. Excitement ran through Laura. She went with John to the estate agent to ask for a viewing. I waited at home for the result.

'Well?' I enquired. I stopped wiping the worktop to watch their expression. John leant back on a base cupboard.

Laura spoke: 'Someone else is interested in it.'

'Are they in a position to buy? Did you ask?'

'No, what do you mean?'

'The purchaser might not have sold their property, but you are ready to buy. Go and knock on the owner's door, explain this, and see what they say.' John went home.

Laura went to the house they had their eye on. 'We can have it.' She reported on her return. She agreed to buy furniture and curtains too. I flung my arms around her.

The mortgage was arranged, and the lenders swallowed our gift of money in the deal. Contracts were signed, and the keys handed over.

Laura and John stepped through their front door. They stepped into their future. When Rob and I visited later that day, John's parents had already arrived. I had brought champagne. I held my glass in the air as tiny bubbles rushed to the top of the glass. 'Here's to Laura and John ... we hope you'll be very happy living here. Cheers.'

We huddled in the kitchen. John's mother stood opposite me, with her arms folded.

'They've done well, haven't they ... buying this house?' I ventured, wanting to connect with the woman who would be my daughter's mother in the eyes of the law.

'There's a lot needs doing, and it's filthy,' The Mother said. 'A new bathroom, for a start; have you seen the state of it?' I had seen the bathroom. There was nothing wrong with the suite or the fittings. 'And it needs a new kitchen.' She sniffed, surveying the room. Releasing her breath, she added, 'And the windows, they all need replacing.'

To our way of thinking, Rob's and mine, the soon-to-be-married couple had a house, the bedrock of married life. Jobs that needed doing could be done in the future, but no, John's mother was adamant.

John's father set to work. The bathroom was ripped out and replaced with a brand-new, white suite. The kitchen cupboards were yanked off and replaced by cream Shaker-style ones. Rob felt obliged to join in the renovations. With spare time shuffled into his busy schedule, he transformed a downstairs cupboard into a cloakroom with a toilet and sink. He fitted a new front door and handed over shiny unused keys. I painted skirting boards and walls. The windows were being replaced by John's dad with help from a mate, John was too busy to assist. Laura remained useless by design, of any practical involvement.

I picked up the telephone. 'Is that Laura's mum?'

'Yes.'

'It's John's dad. I've fallen off the ladder putting an upstairs window in.'

'Oh dear.'

'I think I've broken my leg. Can you take me to the hospital?'

'Yes, I'll be right there.' I approached the house and saw the man with the broken leg lying on the grass, looking even greyer than usual. I pulled to a stop. The mate helped John's dad to stand, and assisted him into my car.

'Go and lock the house,' John's dad said to me, his face deformed by pain.

I took the man with a broken leg to the Accident and Emergency department. I got a wheelchair for him to sit on. 'Don't tell the wife,' he said. 'Her nerves are bad.' I wheeled him to the reception desk. He did not want me to wait, or take him home, and I had no qualms about leaving him.

With a broken leg, John's dad was laid up for months. Rob gained the task of finishing the windows that did not need replacing. The house was near completion.

John's family is of the Catholic faith. They attend church each Sunday. Our faith lies with the Church of England. We do not visit church to keep our religion in check. His family put great importance on their religious beliefs. John's mother has not smoked one cigarette since standing in a sea of people at the Vatican City, adding her voice to the cries of 'Il Papa'. An experience she classified as an audience with the Pope. We offered to hold the wedding at their church, not in the bride's parish as tradition dictates. The ceremony would take place in six months time.

At the same time, Rob and I returned from holiday. Laura greeted us at the door, the trace of tears still visible on her face. 'What's up?' I asked. I put my bag on the floor.

'We went to visit the priest to have a pre-marital lesson. He took me in a room on my own. He demanded I sign a contract.'

'A contract?' Rob asked.

'He wanted me to sign to agree that any children I have will attend a Catholic school. I'm not making that decision now.'

'Why has that upset you?' I asked.

'Because the priest refuses to marry us unless I sign. John's mother is in a rage with me.'

'Sign it,' I said.

'No, I won't be bullied. I'll make my own decision when the time comes.'

The kettle boiled for Rob to make hot drinks. 'Get married in your parish church,' I said. 'I'll contact the vicar tomorrow.'

Laura and I visited the vicar. He agreed to conduct the wedding. There would be a slight change to the original date, but as no invitations had been sent, this was not a problem. Laura and I waltzed out of the vestry, her arm linked through mine.

John's mother frothed at the mouth. She would not set one foot inside a Church of England church. She is of Irish descent and had no tolerance for English custom. John told Laura to cancel the church, he would not go against his mother's wish. The church was cancelled, the wedding was not. John suggested they get married at a registry office.

What did I think of my daughter being pushed around like this? I kept my emotions in check and my mouth shut. I did not want to upset Laura with my take on John and his family.

I searched for a hotel to carry out the ceremony, registry style. A hotel that could accommodate our celebration too. I found a country manor, a huge castle-like building, set in acres of land. The desired date was available. We booked a

38

function room with a balcony overlooking the magnificent greenery. No matter to John's family the marriage would not be sanctioned in a church. We chose good food and wine, champagne on arrival, champagne for the toast. There would be a sit-down wedding breakfast, a disco, and a buffet in the evening.

I made the wedding dress. At the final fitting, I viewed Laura from the full-length mirror on the turn of the stairs. She looked amazing. She was thrilled with her reflection. A column dress, with silver swirls embroidered on white silk, a large bow in the same fabric sat on her back at waist level, with layers of silk netting flowing to form a train. 'You look divine,' I said. She patted her flat stomach and turned sideways for a different view. I blocked out an image slinking into my mind, for it would not happen: her dad walking her down the aisle of a church.

For the bridesmaids, four in all, I made lilac silk column dresses with an overlay of lilac silk chiffon. John, with his copious number of ushers and two best men, hired morning suits. The invitations were in circulation. Just two weeks until the wedding, Rob and I booked a honeymoon for the couple: a surprise gift.

The ring of the telephone filled our empty house. The caller spoke to the answering machine, a message of doom. It waited for my return. The red light of the machine flashed a warning. I switched the knob to play. 'Laura, you think you've the world wrapped up in a rubber band. Well, your boyfriend's seeing someone else. In fact, he's got loads of women.' My heart skipped a beat. I did not erase the message as I wanted Rob to hear it. When he returned home we both stood over the machine and listened in silence. We shared a look. We knew the message to be true. Our daughter was about to marry a serial adulterer.

Laura arrived home, lulled by the train journey from the city. I stretched my arms in front of me and clasped my wrist as if in a cuff. I could not quell the unease creeping into my gut. I let go of my stretch. 'Come and sit down. We have something to tell you.' And we did.

'I want to hear it.' Laura raced to the machine to play the message. She said nothing to Rob or me of what she had heard, whether she believed or not. I told Laura I believed it, with all the shifty behaviour he was capable of. Laura telephoned John and told him of the message. She went to her room and closed the door. She did not want to discuss the ramifications of this information. John arrived within the hour. He stood in the kitchen and told Laura the message was a pack of lies. He bobbed his head around the sitting-room door to tell Rob and me the same. His handsome face was confident and relaxed. He went home. An hour later, Laura grabbed her bag and car key. 'I'm going after him, to his house,' she shouted. The front door slammed.

Anxious for her return, Rob and I waited. A cold stone dropped in my stomach and made a home there. My heart was sprinting, my head ran on two weeks ahead to a wedding in the balance. We heard Laura's car roar up the drive, we heard the car door bang, we listened for her key in the lock, and it turned. 'So?' we asked.

Deflated, Laura sat on the floor by my chair. 'He was in his house with his best friend. I asked whether he had cheated on me. He didn't deny it this time. He said he was sorry. When he's drunk women pester him.'

'Pester him! So what are you going to do?' I asked.

Laura sighed, examined her newly bitten nails. 'His mum arrived, and his friend went home. I asked him to come with me. Live in our house without getting married.'

'And?'

'His mum threw a fit and said he must stay at home with her.'

And that is what John did. The mother of all mothers had won, the boy was hers to keep. Good luck, God bless, Amen. Oh, and good bloody riddance. I looked at Laura sitting on the floor, her legs bent at the knee, her feet in line with her thighs, her position of comfort from being a child. My heart jumped over to her. I was livid, but glad to have my daughter freed from this drip of a lad; though she was devastated and I shared her pain.

Telephone calls were made and wedding arrangements were cancelled. Conversation produced tears between family and friends. Laura's grandma said, 'He must be in that confessional box, bloody morning, noon and night.'

John did not contact Laura. She was bereft. I feared she would be damaged. She had been abandoned, tossed aside without care. Her self-esteem had torn. Laura threw out keepsakes and cleared her 'bottom drawer' of items she had collected for her new life as a married woman.

So was this the turning point? Did this experience turn my daughter into a full-blown alcoholic?

She had taken a step into the arms of alcoholism but full membership was yet to follow.

His greed fed her

Laura completed and passed the nursing course. She was a qualified RGN. I was not made aware that I could have attended graduation, where individual photographs were taken to honour the graduates. Laura robbed me of the keepsake. She applied for a job at the hospital she had trained at, a post in the Medical Assessment Unit, where patients are transferred from Accident and Emergency to wait for a ward specific to their condition. Laura had a career. Her future welcomed her.

She was due to start her new job straight after the now defunct honeymoon. These should have been happy times, reason for rejoicing.

Since John had gone his merry way with his mother, Laura had cried a well of tears. She spent her honeymoon period lying on her bed, or curled on the settee. Days struggled into night, then slipped back into days. Tunes of loss and lyrics of heartache played through her earphones, encouraging more tears to flow. What could I do to ease her sense of loss? Nothing, I was helpless. But as her mum I felt responsible for her return to happiness. The endless cups of tea I offered were left to go cold. My career of being overwhelmed by my daughter's fragile state had begun.

In the immediate aftermath, Laura was not fit for the induction day at the hospital. We headed off, Laura and I, to explain to the ward manager the events which had recently taken place in Laura's life. The manager halted her duties and led us to a quiet room. Laura began to tell her manager of the trauma that had broken her, but tears robbed her statement. I looked at my daughter, then to the woman my daughter needed to impress. I took over and told the manager of the wedding that never was. The manager was understanding and kind. She offered Laura a two-week postponement to the start of her career. She touched Laura's arm and smiled at me. She made her excuses and returned to her busy ward.

Eyes dried, Laura and I stepped out from the artificial light of the hospital into the spring sunshine. Spring that year would not bring a wave of renewal, not for us. We had a job to do in town. We headed to the baker's shop to pay for the uncut wedding cake. Laura halted her stride on the pavement. A tear welled in her eye and spilt onto her cheek. 'I feel lost. I feel as if someone has died.'

'I know.' I put my arms around her. We stood alone among a throng of passersby. 'But there's no sticking plaster for this wound. Time will heal, you'll see. Wait for the pain to pass.' I longed to do something concrete to reduce her suffering, but nothing had broken which I could fix. John would ease Laura's pain, more than he knew.

A 'For Sale' sign appeared outside the vacant, not-to-be-marital home. We had not requested it, we thought it too soon. I contacted the estate agent. John's father had negotiated the asking price, negotiated the terms. He had put the house up for sale. We did not wish to communicate with John, nor his father, and definitely not his mother. We allowed the house sale to go ahead. Laura did not return to that empty house: too many hopes resided there, far fewer memories stayed. Laura recalled what happened on Valentine's Day. John's father had taken a card, and a bottle of wine, then placed them on the bedroom floor of the empty house for Laura to discover. My eyebrows ascended at this disclosure. Notwithstanding the pain my daughter was going through, I was glad she was not marrying this boy.

Rob and I entered the redundant house for sale to tidy the loose ends of renovation. A phantom house, I imagined my daughter's vision of happiness within these walls, and my heart raced over to hers. The empty house echoed our footsteps while we carried out the work needed. We loaded the van with a freezer from the garage. I turned the new key in the lock for the last time. I brought home paint brushes and chucked them in the bin.

The house soon sold. A stranger would benefit from the false love poured into that property. The house had risen in value, down to renovations and a market boom. After taking out Laura's investment, the money Rob and I had given her, there would be a healthy profit for the ex-couple to share. We instructed a solicitor. I said we, I meant me. Laura was not good at this sort of thing, and Rob was busy with work.

There had been no legal joining of the couple, and they had never lived together. And, my daughter was the injured party in the breakdown of the relationship. 'Surely,' I said to the solicitor, 'the money we invested in the house belongs to my daughter?' The solicitor agreed.

John received notice of Laura's intention to claim back her inheritance. Laura received communication from his solicitor: John would not accept the request for the refund of our investment, and wanted half of all proceeds. He and his family had acquired a taste for crisp bank notes; the shared money from the rise in value of the property was not enough. Official letters pigeoned back and forth. We waited for a resolution, and time crept by. The money Rob and I had squirrelled away, worked hard for to secure our daughter's future, sat waiting for a decision of ownership.

Laura and I made an appointment to visit the solicitor to find out why it was taking so long to finalise the sale of the house. 'John may have a case,' the solicitor said, 'as you did not stipulate ownership of the money when the contracts were signed.' My mouth fell open. The solicitor continued, and my ears buzzed with the tone of her voice. 'Employ a barrister, and take the matter to court. I am sure you have a case.' Laura and I walked home, stunned into silence.

The reason we did not put a clause in the contract to ring-fence the money belonging to Laura? She was to be a wife and John our son, in the eyes of the law. We did not treat our daughter as separate from him, not wanting to tip the scales of their union by making Laura wealthier. We made no stipulation when the house was purchased, when contracts were signed, when keys were handed over. We made no stipulation that Laura invested money, and he did not.

Back home, I told Rob the recommendation of the solicitor. 'What do you think?' I asked.

Rob stopped the job he was doing. He looked at Laura, knowing she had no funds. 'I'm not paying for a barrister. Enough money has flown down that drain.' Still looking at his daughter, his chin rippled. He gently shook his head.

Traitorous John hid behind his mother, hid behind his father, hid behind his solicitor. Behind the comfort of these shields, he was confident he was entitled to half our investment. And half our investment he got: he stole. Laura grew stronger fed by his greed.

To cheer Laura, Rachael and I took her shopping in the city. And of all the people to bump into, to see across a crowded street: John with his sister, pushing a trolley with a child in, the child he said was not his. We shared no communication, not even a glare. Driving home, we passed John's car which had broken down at the traffic lights. Rachael peeped her horn. Laura drew comfort from that.

The time had come for Laura to put on her nurse's uniform, her mascara and lipstick, and report for work. Her new life had begun. I relaxed. I was happy for her. She bought new clothes, partied with friends new and old. She had recovered, and blossomed again, such a striking, attractive girl. I know all mothers think that of their child, but she was. She was stunning, with her jet hair, jewelled blue eyes, flawless skin, and a figure shaped to perfection. I felt a sense of relief. My former self had returned.

Laura loved being a nurse. She had found her calling, she excelled in her job. Friends of friends reported Laura's value when dealing with their loved ones as patients. Sadly, Laura's career as an alcoholic was also about to begin.

Alcohol and medics

Things I did not know back then: there is a prevalence of medics who become alcoholics and drug addicts.

I read somewhere that medical students are consistent with their peers in using alcohol and drugs. But a higher pattern of addiction is apparent when medics increase in age, in comparison with other professions.

Why is this so? Is it because medics work irregular hours and no two working weeks are the same? Typically, social intake of alcohol is at the weekend or in an evening. Medics work weekends, they work nights. Their pattern of socialising is disrupted. Any day becomes a drink day, any time of day becomes a drink hour. If any day, any hour is acceptable for the consumption of alcohol, it is more likely that one drinking day leaks into another. When the time to drink alcohol has no boundaries, a habit is formed. I think of Laura's drinking in the mornings, at lunch time, through the night. Should Laura have taken the office job offered in her youth? If she were shackled to a desk each working day she would not be able to pour bottles of wine down her throat at three o'clock in the afternoon.

Could immersion in duty be responsible for the rise in alcohol consumption in the medical profession? Medics visit disease daily. Patients die beyond a medic's capability. Medics handle corpses; they look into dead eyes. They live with stress daily. Alcohol and drugs may be used to relieve stress, as a coping mechanism.

Are medics flippant with their own health? Medics are familiar with drugs, the power to ease pain and enhance life. The spike of a needle, the swallowing of a tablet, medics are experienced in such activity. Medics witness recovery from drugs, they are aware drugs can mask a symptom. Do medics take for granted nature's ability to restore? Are they seduced by their knowledge of what a drug is capable of?

Laura was emotionally damaged. She belonged to the profession of medics. Two factors in the consideration of what makes a person an addict. She would meet a third factor, and a fourth.

If I had known this equation back then, could I have steered my daughter away from alcoholism, prevented her from taking drugs? With experience, I know I could not have saved her. All warnings, all pleadings, all evidence of the utter despair of a mother losing her daughter, did nothing to halt Laura's destructive nature. I cried down the telephone. I sobbed into the ear of my morbid, drunk daughter, with no response.

How do you stop a freight train along its journey? You stand in front of the propelled force, you sacrifice yourself. I became wise over the years: you cannot prevent a person along their journey of self-destruction.

In hope, we moved on.

Champagne lifestyle

Laura met a nice boy. A boy from a family we knew, a boy with a future and a past.

She bounced into our bedroom early one Saturday morning and sat on the end of the bed. 'Guess what?' she beamed.

'What?' I pulled the duvet away from my face; Rob did not.

47

'I met Dan last night. He's asked me out on a date.' I sat up to this piece of news.

'That's wonderful, much better suited to you than John.'

'I agree. You know, Mum, I think I was more in love with the thought of being married than in love with John.' Laura left our bedroom and went back to her own. I snuggled next to Rob under the covers.

'Well, that is good news,' I said. I slung my legs over the side of the bed and got up, and went downstairs to switch on the kettle. A smile lit my eyes, and stayed a while.

Dan took Laura to an unusual restaurant. He held her hand across a candlelit table. I crossed my fingers, I crossed my toes. Dan was the tonic Laura needed.

Laura's socialising was no longer confined to weekends as shift patterns at the hospital took care of that. She returned home one Thursday lunch after spending the previous night out. Usually, Laura preferred home and her own bed. A taxi door would slam. Her heels would click-clack their staccato beat up the drive. Laura's, or Rachael's key would slide in the lock, and inside either one of them would step. Then I could sleep. If Laura was absent from her bed, as on the previous evening, there was a reason. And that reason was carved over her face: she had been drinking alcohol to excess. She ran upstairs to be with me. 'Mum, I won't be seeing Dan again. I slept with him last night.'

'That's because you were pissed!' Disappointment heightened my temper. 'You're a disgrace.'

Laura went on to tell me that after sleeping with him, she made demands of him. Demands he was unprepared to give.

'Well, you've blown that then, haven't you?'

'I'll never get drunk again,' she said, and promised not to leave herself vulnerable in the hands of alcohol ever again.

The following week Laura came home drunk. She spent all Sunday in bed. At four o'clock in the afternoon, I entered her bedroom. I sat by her bed and lectured her. I left the door open and told her to get up. She did not. Downstairs, I told Rob of the previous week's incident: sleeping with Dan. I expected him to join in my concern and discuss how we could help stop our daughter losing her way. He got out of his chair, charged up the stairs, called his daughter a whore and told her to get out of bed. I was ashamed for telling him, for betraying my daughter's confidence. 'Why did you tell Dad?' Her question dangled in the air, for I had no excuse to make.

I did not know whether Dan held the key to my daughter's happiness. I clutched at possibilities and snatched at a brighter future for her, a better state of emotion for myself.

Rob was told by Dan's brother that Laura had been good for Dan. He had just come out of a long-term relationship and was grieving. Dating someone as gorgeous as Laura had restored his morale. 'Oh, well, I'm glad she's been of service,' I said. I stacked the dishwasher and clattered the mugs together.

Then Laura joined a gym. Kitted herself out in Lycra. Scooped her shiny jet hair into a swishy ponytail. She took a bottle of water out of the fridge and went to exercise. Laura was fit, healthy and beautiful. Unfortunately, the gym provided hospitality to the third factor in the predisposition to becoming an alcoholic: a controlling partner.

Welcome to the charismatic and tall James: the mind bender. He would infiltrate Laura's mind, and cause her harm. He spotted her the second she entered the gym. Before she even began a workout he had asked her for a date.

If you look at a photograph of my daughter snapped in the company of others, you would be drawn to her. Her good looks would pop off the page. Unfortunately, these stunning qualities contributed to her downfall. If Laura had been plain, James would have passed her by.

Laura returned home and told Rachael, also a gym member, of the invitation. 'No,' Rachael said. 'He's an arsehole, he treats women like crap.'

James approached Rachael in the gym, told her he would be the one to treat her sister right. 'Prove it,' Rachael challenged. 'Take her somewhere nice.' To the seaside Laura and James went for the day. They held hands, shared ice cream, and came home before dark. James carried on doing special things, carried on treating Laura right. She was smitten. He said he had suffered heartache, and understood Laura's vulnerable side. He said he was an only child and his parents had been killed in a plane crash. We did not know he told lies and painted pictures for sympathy to form a connection. He drew illusions to lure women, gullible women. Reciprocation: I need you, you need me. The first stage of entrapment.

James had a house, a starter home, where Laura spent time. He had bigger plans, and laid a deposit on a detached new-build. He wanted Laura to go through the brand-new entrance and live with him. 'It's only been four months since the wedding was cancelled,' I reminded Laura. 'All that upset! Give yourself time to recover, to be sure you're doing the right thing.' I did not want a cloud of heartache to park over my daughter's head again.

With a frown on her brow and a petulant lip, she agreed. But added, 'James doesn't like to come home to an empty house. He doesn't like to live alone.'

Laura mentioned a strange thing. 'James' parents were divorced. He had lots of sisters.'

'I thought you said he was an only child, and his parents were dead; killed in a plane crash.'

'That's what he told me. Must have been a misunderstanding.'

'I don't like the sound of that.'

Laura had no further comment. She realised she had said too much. Rob and I shared concern over this news, our alarm bells chimed. But our daughter was magnetised to the lifestyle offered by James. She brushed away the vile tale of dead parents.

James' house sold, but the new-build was not ready. He moved into his, very much alive, father's house. Simultaneously, Rob and I were set to jet off abroad. Before suitcases left the hall, Laura asked, 'Can James stay here with me, until you get back? He doesn't like living with his dad.'

'No,' Rob and I chirped. Rob added, 'We haven't even met the lad.'

Rob and I returned home from holiday late at night, tanned and tired. Laura jumped out of bed and ran down the stairs to greet us. Said how much she had missed us. This was a disguise to cover her guilt. As the week rolled on, I discovered clues left by James of his week's stay in our home. He wanted it known: our daughter had betrayed her mum and dad. I left this fact unsaid.

James supplied Laura with weekends in the city, expensive hotels, VIP tickets to nightclubs and a taxi on account to take a princess out and bring her home again. A fistful of money was pressed into her waiting hand. Laura loved this lifestyle. Oh, how she loved it. She was unaware that women before her, women who would follow, also enjoyed his lifestyle. Laura was led to believe she was the only one.

Hollow proposal

Rob and I had gifted both daughters a deposit for a house. Both daughters were to be married that year, now only one. Rachael chose Laura to be her chief bridesmaid. I made Rachael's dress: white silk, embossed with white flowers, a bodice laced at the back with a modesty inlay, a long full skirt with a bustle at the back. An underskirt made of layers of silk netting to puff the skirt out. The bridesmaids wore white silk long column skirts, a bodice with a panel of blue silk embroidered flowers at the front. The groom wore a Scottish traditional suit with a kilt. His Scottish, extended, family arrived and walked up the road to the church. They looked amazing in their traditional regalia.

A gifted sunny day greeted the wedding party for my youngest daughter. Laura smiled for the cameras, stood in line when asked. But her face showed no happiness for her sister. Rachael floated through the day, enjoyed every second. A radiant, photogenic, pretty blonde bride – beautiful.

At the wedding breakfast, Laura sat at the long table by my side. The bride and groom sat in the middle of the same table. Laura lifted a glass of wine to her lips. She drank some, not all. My shoulders released their tension.

James attended the wedding, after much persuasion. He arrived in his prestige car. He wore a designer suit with a crisp white shirt. A heavy gold watch strapped to his wrist. He would not mingle, or even raise a glass. Rachael asked him to join her in dance: he refused. He sat at the table assigned to him and watched people interact. A smile never did shimmy his lips. He encouraged Laura to leave the celebration before the wedding cake was cut. He wanted to retire to the hotel suite, funded by Rob and me. We thought we understood: it was hard for Laura to share Rachael's wedding day less than six months after her own had been cancelled. We understood nothing. Laura's demeanour was the result of being bullied by James. He disliked the bond she shared with her family, and he had a plan to break that bond. He laid out his intention before her, but she did not see the red line of action to isolate her.

Money, a considerable sum, sat in Laura's bank account. Although she had lost the money we gave her, there were funds from the sale of the house. Proceeds from the marriage that never was. Rob and I took Laura to a new housing estate. We viewed a house near to completion. We encouraged Laura to buy it and offered support with the finance. 'And my daughter can choose the cupboards and the tiles?' I asked the lady who fluttered around us. A smile and affirmative nod were given. 'Look, Laura. Which colour scheme would you like?'

Laura lacked excitement. I sensed she was nervous of taking on the commitment alone. A deposit held the plot in Laura's name.

'It's an investment,' Rob said to Laura. He and I were pleased.

At this time, Laura was a committed nurse, she attended shifts at varying times. Rob and I came home early one summer evening. Laura was in bed, retired early in preparation for her shift the next day. I popped my head round her bedroom door. She asked for a glass of fresh orange, then gulped it down. We chatted for a few minutes. 'We've been to a beer festival,' she said. She was referring to

53

James. I kissed her forehead, took the empty glass, and closed her bedroom door.

The next day a tale came my way: Laura was paralytic at the beer festival. 'Is this true?' I asked her.

'No, you saw me last evening. Did I seem drunk to you?' I dismissed the tale as an act of jealousy. The same person saw James walking in a direction that made no sense.

I think of the orange juice, the need to drink it all at once. I think of James, and the direction his womanising took. I look back and wonder: What was fact? What was fiction?

Laura and I began to see the world differently. The volume of our arguments increased. She was snappy and self-obsessed. She had acquired an arrogance I did not recognise. She came into the house, the home she loved to be in, to say hi then bye. 'How's it going?' I asked. She was vague. She used to tell me all, included me in this and that. 'Talk to me,' I said. She squirmed. She did not have the time. 'You've changed,' I remarked. This argument had wings and it flew: it seemed I did not like her enjoying herself. I did not like that she had a life.

As a parent you are warned to look for signs of change in your child's behaviour and personality; a strong indication the child may be consuming drugs. The thought never crossed my mind. Laura was not a child – she was twenty-five years old.

Seeds sown by James started to grow. Little shoots of discontent. Family life was to be laughed at, derided as pathetic. Laura now viewed her family time, her bond with us, through his eyes. He demanded it so. There was a problem for the couple: my unwillingness to give my blessing to Laura moving in with him. She resolved it: stoked and prodded an altercation until it blew. We had an audience that day: Rob. I still hear her words today, see her cold blue eyes directed at her dad, when she said, 'You have no idea how vindictive she is when you're not here.'

'How dare you!' I spat. Our emotions grew out of control.

'That's it,' Rob declared. He returned Laura's cold stare. 'Pack your bags and go.' Her bags were half packed. Rob said I was complicit: 'Six-of-one and half-a-dozen of the other.' Laura grabbed a few things. She stormed out of the house with a smile on her face. Said she would be back to collect the rest of her belongings. It broke Rob's heart to throw his daughter out of our home. We were bereft. He had tossed her out, we had let her down. I was frustrated with her behaviour, but now she had gone, I stared out of the window, already missing her. My lovely daughter who used to be my friend.

The next morning, birds chirped their morning song. From the kitchen window, I watched them eat nuts from a cage hammered into the trunk of our tree. James' prestige car backed up the drive. He sat in the driving seat. The boot of the car opened automatically to take Laura's things away. Laura appeared in the hall, used her key to open my door. 'Any bin bags?' she asked. Where was her sense of remorse? Words of sorrow for the way she had treated me? She ran upstairs to cram her stuff into the gaping mouth of black bin liners. I took a bottle of champagne out of the fridge and held it. The cold glass helped synchronise my feelings. Up and down the stairs Laura hurtled. The prestige car's boot swallowed the bulging black bags. Laura came to the kitchen: she came to say goodbye. I held out the unopened bottle of champagne.

'Be happy,' I said. I held back tears, she would not have time to console me, not with James waiting in the car. She was stepping into the life she wanted, and for that much I was happy. The front door closed. I watched through the window as she bounced into the passenger seat. The blast of the car's exhaust pipes trumpeted my daughter's departure.

After living with James for a few months, Laura invited Rob and me to Sunday dinner, to the house shared with James. She was duty bound to us. It was late afternoon when we arrived, and Laura was still in bed. James had a broad smile on his face. Rob and I sat on the white leather settee, waiting for our daughter to put in an appearance. The meal was prepared by a supermarket. We sat around the glass dining table to dine on lamb, to spoon on mint sauce. Laura and her beau sat facing Rob and me. She complained of being hot. James dabbed his forehead with the palm of his hand. They shared a look that excluded us, and they struggled to eat their meal. James had a tale to tell: our daughter had vomited in the garden at three o'clock that morning. After expelling her greedy intake, she composed herself, went back in the house and shared a bottle of vodka with him as they watched the sun peep over the horizon. Rob and I glanced at each other with a shared look of concern. James aired a second tale: Laura's lump sum of money in her bank account had dwindled. We chastised her, reminding her the money was the deposit for a mortgage on her new-build, not to be spent on frippery. Laura denied the tale of spending, and we believed her. We thought him odd, telling tales of our daughter. We did not consider our daughter had become adept at telling lies.

James would engineer a rift between my daughter and me. He hacked a chasm in our mother-and-daughter relationship, then chased it into an abyss.

Laura's new-build house was near completion. Rob and I were due to fly abroad for leisure. The contracts for Laura's house would be exchanged while we were on holiday.

56

On our return, I opened the front door. We dragged suitcases into the hall and warmed the house with lighting. We retired to bed, happy with our lot.

In the morning, Rob left for work with a kiss planted on my cheek, a lunchbox tucked under his arm. I loaded the washing machine. Midmorning, Laura arrived. 'We had a brilliant holiday,' I said. I would have liked to tell her more, sharing the fun and the experiences, but she cut me short.

'I've pulled out of buying the house,' she said.

'What? Why?'

'I want to stay with James. He wants me to invest my money in his house.'

'I bet he does.'

'I knew you'd be like this. I'm not giving him the money. My name will go on the deeds. Anyway, it will be better for you and Dad.'

'How's that then?'

'You won't have to lend me money'.

'I bet this idea was his. Why didn't you wait till Dad and I got home from holiday before making this decision?' Though I knew the reason.

'Whether you like it or not, I'm living with James. And he says it makes sense to invest the money with him.'

I told Rob of our daughter's investment swap when he came home. He closed his eyes and rocked his head, his mouth a tight line no words could escape.

I learnt from Laura the terms of her venture into James' property. The house was jointly owned by Laura and him. He had organised life assurance policies on each other. My mind tumbled these policies: Had James included Laura in home ownership to put a price on her life? To take out insurance on her longevity? I asked Laura to cancel the policy with her name on. She declined. Further down the line, when their relationship began to split at the seam, she passed this tidbit to me: 'I have to pay him.'

'Pay him for what?'

'To live in that house.'

'How much?'

'Five hundred pounds a month.'

'Five hundred!'

A look of withdrawal ran through her eyes. A look I was familiar with. She changed tack. 'Yes, but that covers everything, food, even the cleaner's wage.'

'The cleaner's wage! Good grief, why can't you two clean the house?'

'He doesn't want to.' I had received a snippet of truth, a slice of discontent. But, if I challenged her to change her life, she clamped her mouth, and her eyes danced with lies.

Laura applied for promotion and a move from the hectic hospital ward she loved. It would take her away from varied staff to a sedate nursing home with fewer people to mingle with. She practised interview techniques, she put on a show for me. 'If I get this job, I'll earn more money, I'll be on a higher band.'

'But you love being at the hospital.'

'I know, but this will be a challenge. Doctors are not always on the premises, so a nurse has more responsibility. Anyway, James wants me to earn more money.'

How strange: Mr James Look How Rich I Am was short of money? No, he was suspicious of the varied staff Laura mingled with. The patients she came to meet. The doctors who might catch her eye. A nursing home would reduce the contact of people Laura may have a giggle with. Laura was offered the position. She left the hospital and began work at the nursing home.

One day, I came out of the supermarket loaded with groceries. I saw Laura across the car park. She walked towards me. 'Shouldn't you be in work?'

'I've come for teabags for the ward.' Bags under her eyes soaked her sparkle.

'You don't look well. Is everything all right?'

'Can I come and see you after my shift? I can't talk now.'

'Of course.'

She lent to me, and I kissed her cheek. I walked away from her, and carried the heavy bags, with a load on my mind.

With spiralling anguish I waited for Laura. When she arrived I pushed a coffee in her hand. 'So what's wrong?' I closed the door and followed her into the sitting-room.

'Nothing's wrong; just thought I'd pop in and see you.' Much of what Laura said did not make sense. I knew she was lying and that she had a problem of some kind. She had simply changed her mind about sharing with me. She was not ready to let me into her world.

I would visit Laura at the pristine house when James was not home. All furniture, wall hangings, cream carpets (shoes off at the door) were chosen by him and belonged to him. Laura owned one designer bowl; it was on display.

Something in the air, undiscovered, lurked in that house. I could taste it, I could feel it. It was a house, not a home.

It was to be our first Christmas without resident daughters. I shopped with Laura for an artificial Christmas tree for the house she shared. Pine needles on the carpet would not be acceptable. The fake tree came complete with baubles. I helped her erect the green branches onto the unblemished carpet. We stood back and admired the complete token of Christmas. A touch of warmth in a cold house.

Rob and I threw a party on Christmas Eve. Laura arrived with James later than everyone else. Her hair was just so; she wore an expensive mini skirt and stilettos with straps to match. I rubbed her cold arm and handed her a drink. After the party, the girls clambered into a shared taxi to go to town: Laura, James, Rachael, and Barry. Their destination reached, they all piled out. James steered Laura away from Rachael. Unlike the old days, the girls went their separate ways. James liked a crowd to stand out in. He wanted people to envy him. Laura's beauty endorsed his status.

Rob and I visited Laura on Christmas morning to take our gifts to her. She was dressed in uniform. A hangover clung to her face. I handed James a present, out of respect to our daughter. He ripped open the wrapping and took out the designer jacket. He smiled a smile that did not raise his cheeks. Boxing Day, the zip was broken on the designer jacket, the teeth were pulled apart. James could not wait to tell me: the gift was of no use to him.

I wonder if Laura went to work that Christmas Day, or had she put on her uniform to fool us? The Christmas tree was the perfect symbol of her artificial life.

Not long after Christmas, the daughter I had concern for telephoned me. 'Mum, can I come back home, to live?'

'Yes, but ...'

'Can you come and help with my stuff before he gets back?'

I set out to her rescue the moment the call ended, happy to take her away from that cruel man. We stuffed those bulging black bin bags into the boot of my car. Her car was fully loaded. She told me she had had enough of his cruelty, enough of his womanising. Laura backed her car onto the street, and I aimed mine homeward.

Her bedroom sat in wait with the duvet pulled back. The kettle boiled. We sat down and had a chat. James had pulled her hair. 'A fistful,' she said. I searched her scalp for an absent bald patch. She had hidden behind the front door, waiting for his key to turn in the lock. She aimed a can of hairspray and sprayed the sticky mist into his shocked eyes. Had he been caught cheating? No, worse than that: he paraded his conquests. He made sure Laura suffered his joy. He told Laura he had a gorgeous blonde model. 'And d'you know what? She looked just like your mum, but taller.' I wondered just what kind of person would encourage a daughter to be jealous of her own mother.

Our problem daughter, back home to stay, was treated like a guest. There was no evidence of heartbreak, no spilling of tears. Rob and I assumed her to be happy to be parted from James. We thought wrong. On day one of the exodus from the shared house, James had sat in his plush car and waited for Laura outside the nursing home. They were a couple still. Her departure had simply been a ploy to gain attention from him. After a few respectful days of our hospitality, she confessed to their reunion and moved back in

61

with him. We could not stop her going, we could not hold her back. The black bags, not yet unpacked, went back to the lonely, cold house. James bought Laura a gift to thank her for coming back, an expensive gift to smear over a crack. Weekends were their problem, she said. Weekdays were just fine: they shared humour, snuggled in front of the television, drank a bottle of wine. He would not allow Laura to drink alcohol on a Friday night because he had jobs to do. He lathered his body with fake tan, prepared himself for his Saturday night, which was his time to do as he pleased. He bought a crate of wine from the Cash and Carry to keep Laura at home on these Saturday nights.

Laura left James several times. Each occasion brought our daughter back home. We welcomed her with problems and heartache accruing. I would arrive home and see Laura's car on the drive, black bin bags shoved on the back seat. 'Not again,' my mouth said to my sinking heart.

We had words, Laura and I: 'Come away for good.'

'I have. I'm not going back, ever.'

'Mmm … if he had no money, if he drove an old banger, would you be messing around like this?' She had no answer. James had a powerful hold on my daughter.

I did not see a new addiction creep in. I thought her vulnerable, brought on by rejection. It took years for me to realise my daughter had become addicted to drama. She got a kick out of the attention a crisis brought. A cocktail of emotions she desired. Jitters in her stomach curbed her appetite for food. She embraced the stir of jealousy, an emotion she came to crave. Laura acquired a weapon to fight back: she copied his behaviour, seeking attention from other men. She inflamed the strain of jealousy, taking pleasure from making James cry.

By now, Laura was engulfed in an abusive relationship: mental abuse. Her self-concept and independence were systematically being chipped away. Like my daughter, James had a personality disorder, he had a feeling of entitlement and privilege. He enjoyed power.

The relationship between Laura and James continued. Their union did not end, it changed. James upped the stakes in their struggle for supremacy. And he won. He knew Laura could handle his one-night-stands, so now he brought home a woman named Sheena, who he intended to keep. He was thrilled to walk down the High Street knowing two women grasped for his favour.

Sheena's mother worked in a supermarket, the one where I shopped. I had chatted with this woman in the past, compared the trial of being a mother to young adults. One day, she sought me out at the bakery section. She gushed: her daughter had connected with James. 'Just a moment,' I said. 'Laura has a relationship with him.' Sheena's mother told me he really loved her daughter. He had offered her daughter a job. To some people, James was a desirable prospect. He had a presence, he had a business, oh, and yes, he had money. 'Well, I hope it works out for her,' I said. And I did hope that. Let this mother and her daughter have the arsehole, and let my daughter step out of this hideous relationship.

Months tripped by. Sheena's mother paused the stacking of shelves. I walked past her. She caught my ear and told a tale I did not like. Laura had entered the house she had invested money in with James. Pushed her key into the lock in the middle of the night. She stepped into the unlit hall. She made her way to her bedroom. Sheena was in bed with James. An almighty row kicked off when the two women collided. Sheena phoned her parents, she wanted them to support her. The parents did as they were bid. They drove their car to the discontented house and waited outside. Laura knew better than to ring Rob or me in the early hours of the morning to sort out an argument she knew we would not approve of. Laura was chucked out of her house that night. Left to find her way home to us. Sheena's mother admitted she no longer admired James. She shared her distaste for the rolling story of his alive, dead parents. When she had finished venting, I told her Laura owned half the house her daughter slept in. 'Oh, I didn't know that,' she said. I skidded home to confront my daughter. I abandoned the groceries in the car. I flung open the front door and stepped into the house. Unsuspecting, Laura lay in a bath of bubbles. I raced upstairs and screeched at her through the bathroom door. I raged about the tale I had just heard. The bathroom door opened. Laura, wrapped in a towel with beads of water resting on her suntanned arms, sidled past me and went to her room to connect to James via her mobile phone. Conversation over, and without speaking with me, she re-immersed herself in bubbles.

Ten minutes flashed by. I slammed tins of food in the cupboard, I shoved meat in the freezer. The prestige car purred up the drive and parked. James got out in his pin-striped suit. He gave a firm rat-a-tat-tat on my door. 'What do you want?' I asked. I held the door ajar to avoid him stepping in.

'To see Laura.'

'You can't. She's in the bath.'

He delivered a cold stare, much meaner than mine. 'You can't stop me from seeing her.' Defeated, I stepped aside and let him in. He took the stairs two at a time. He was invited into the bathroom by a slide of the lock. I took refuge in the kitchen. I did not want to hear the bilge trickle from his mouth. A half hour staggered by. James boomed down the stairs. No sooner had he slammed the front door behind him than I ran upstairs to hear what happened.

'Everything's sorted,' Laura said. 'He's going to have a word with Sheena about her mother.'

'And what about the dead parent tale? He treats all you women the same. He's a dangerous man.'

'He's just asked me to marry him.' In the mist of the steam, and bubbles-a-popping, this horrid man had proposed to Laura to defuse the situation.

'Pathetic,' I said. I slammed the bathroom door and opened it to slam it again. 'What's wrong with you? Can't you see what an arsehole he is?' I marched to the kitchen for a glass of water and two painkillers.

The proposal of marriage amounted to nothing. No ring to sparkle and shine on the third finger of Laura's left hand. Several proposals of marriage flew Laura's way from the mouth of James. With each invitation to live happily ever after, till death do them part, came a condition: she had to lose weight. Her skin wrapped her bones like cling film, what weight could she lose? At her thinnest, he informed Laura he preferred a woman with curves. Mind games, and there were a lot. We were escalating to dangerous times.

Laura's birthday, her twenty-seventh: she was at the height of her beauty, and her skin glowed. Her jet hair was fashionably cut, her makeup applied to perfection. She stood in my hall. 'Your aunty has brought a present for you,' I said. 'Where were you?' Laura had known her aunt was going to visit.

'I've been to my house.' The house shared with James. 'My key wouldn't turn. I can't believe he's changed the lock. I was rocking.'

'Laura, for heaven's sake, come away from that man.' She did not take in what I said.

'I jumped over the gate and went to the back door. I knew Sheena was in there, in my house.'

'I can't understand why you invest time in that horrible man.' Still, she was not listening.

'I smashed the kitchen window and climbed in.'

'Laura!'

'I shocked the pair of them. Who does she think she is?'

'Have you cut yourself?' She pulled the sleeves of her black knit up to her elbow, to check her arms: not a scratch.

'What's she done?' Rob shouted.

'Smashed a window at her house,' I replied.

Rob appeared next to Laura and me. 'What the hell are you playing at?' he asked.

'I couldn't get in … and why should she be in there all smug with him?'

I looked at Laura, her lovely face. 'Why are you wasting your life on him?' She shrugged, putting up the barrier she operated when challenged.

'Stop bringing this shit to our door,' Rob said. Her ears locked out good sense.

'Go on,' I said. 'Piss off. I'm sick of it.' Laura left the house, the door slammed behind her. She got in her car and zoomed down the drive.

The day turned into evening, then night appeared. There was no sign of Laura. Messages left on her voice mail went unanswered. Rob and I climbed into bed. The unease we felt spread between us. Rob lay on his side, on his back, on his other side, pulling the duvet with him. He picked up his mobile phone to connect with his daughter. He left message after message for his darling girl to call back.

In the early hours and wide awake in bed, Rob and I drank tea to keep our minds occupied. Where was she? Was she safe? Was she alone, or with others? Had we forced a split in her obviously breaking heart? Would she do something stupid? We did not know. Dark shadows of night departed when daylight filled our room.

The doorbell chimed. On jellied legs I rushed to let the outside in, not knowing what I would find. I opened the door to Laura. She was shivering with the booze she had left behind. Relief snatched my anger. I made hot drinks. I steered her into the sitting room. She had spent the previous evening in a restaurant with friends and red wine. She stayed the night at a friend's house, ignoring her dad's plea to return his calls.

The three of us shared a sensible pow-wow. Her behaviour was dissected. We discussed the need for her to change the way she was living. She should start anew, away from the influence of James. Rob recommended she withdraw her name from the deeds of their house and reclaim her funds. We offered money to buy a house between the three of us, a house she could call her home. The morning slipped into afternoon. Hungover and exhausted, Laura needed her bed. Worn out from worry, Rob and I hooked up with the daily grind that had awaited our late start.

It was decided that Laura and I visit a solicitor, who wrote to James, outlining Laura's intention to withdraw from her commitment to the house. James welcomed the request to take Laura off the deed entitlement. To our surprise, he readily paid back the money Laura had deposited into the joint mortgage. I thought he wanted to show money was nothing to him. I thought wrong. He still had a strong hold on Laura. He would not let her go.

My daughter and I went to the estate agent. For sale: a two-bedroom, three-storey modern house with skylights and a courtyard. Without solicitor involvement, Rob, Laura and I made a verbal contract between us. We worked out a percentage of ownership equating to the money each one put in. Rob and I took out the mortgage. Laura would pay a small amount of rent to help with the cost. The house was purchased.

With paint brushes and carpet cleaner, I went to spruce up the place. Laura promised to help, but ran errands instead. We bought furniture. We bought mirrors to reflect happy times. Rachael brought an empty wine-rack to fill a nook. Laura had a parking space in the courtyard and parked her car in that.

Laura had everything: her own home, a career, money in her purse, friends and a supportive family. And yet? It was all nothing, because Sheena now resided with James. We had bought a light and sunny house to welcome our lonely and secretly depressed girl.

My daughter had no experience of living on her own. Rachael bought a kitten to keep her sister company. Keith Smudge was the name Laura gave to this fluffy ball of fun. He was cute. We thought the kitten would be joyful, something to come home to, and be cared for. We were all excited for the new addition and introduced ourselves to the little cat. The pet shop beckoned. I bought what was needed for a kitten's habitat. One whole night, Laura kept him. Keith Smudge shot under her bed, hissed and arched his back. Laura could not handle him. The responsibility, the patience needed, was not for her. She wanted 'it' to go back. Back to where he came from went Keith Smudge, where a new name waited for him. We stood in the courtyard and waved him goodbye.

Laura's wine rack was empty, it did not look the part. I bought six bottles of wine, three red, three white. I thought it would be inviting to offer a visitor a drink. I stood in Laura's kitchen a couple of days later, the wine rack was devoid of all the bottles purchased. With my heart beating a little too fast, I casually asked, 'Have you had company?'

'No, why?'

'No reason.' I looked away from the redundant wine-rack, its chrome wire holding fresh air, with a frown on my brow, and an uneasy feeling which flooded my heart.

A week later, Rob came home from work livid. He had a tale to tell. Laura, with a friend as a passenger, drove to a takeaway pizza place and ordered food to be delivered. She then stepped outside and swayed to her car, pulled open the driver's door, and plonked herself in the seat. She drove away. The delivery man, holding boxes of pizza high in the air, knocked on Laura's door, no answer. The pizza establishment was a customer of ours. The next day, the server rang Rob and told him what she had witnessed, saying Laura appeared to have been drunk. I telephoned Laura at work and asked her to drop by on her way home. It was unusual for me to trouble her at work, so I told her the reason. She did not deny drink-driving. Laura drove her car up the drive and yanked the handbrake on. I waited outside. I snatched the keys from her. I unhooked the car key and handed the bunch of keys back. 'Walk home,' I said, 'and on your way home, call into the pizza place and pay what you owe.'

'You can't do that. I need the car for work.'

69

I was beyond the want to argue. 'Get the bus.' Laura followed me into the house. She sat on the bottom stair. 'You've got to stop this excessive drinking. You're drinking every night, aren't you?' She did not answer. 'Let this be a lucky escape.'

She agreed to drink alcohol only at weekends. She agreed to never get in the car after drinking alcohol. She would let her shoes transport her home.

Rachael had a delightful West Highland White Terrier pup. We had all fallen in love with him. Later that day, I told Rachael about Laura's drink-driving. Rachael was concerned and went to visit her sister. She knocked on Laura's door, and knocked for a second time. Laura opened the door but did not invite Rachael in. The puppy dog got excited on seeing Laura, and struggled to be set free from Rachael's arms. The pup ran in a figure of eight around the courtyard. Laura closed the door and left her pregnant sister to chase and catch the beloved pooch. Rachael came to see Rob and me and told us what had occurred, adding that Laura appeared to have been drunk. Infuriated after our sensible chit-chat that afternoon, Rob and I pulled on shoes. We shot in the car to see Laura, to see if her odd behaviour was the result of alcohol. We left Rachael and the pup to wait for our return. Laura opened her door with a glass of wine in her hand. I snatched the glass from her and flung the liquid at her face. We pushed past her, then went up the stairs to the first landing. Laura's friend from schooldays sat on the floor by the coffee table. A Chinese meal lay on the table, a bottle of wine a centrepiece. Laura's friend, Lyndsey, stood to attention when Rob and I barged in. Lyndsey was aghast to see Laura's parents treat their daughter this way. 'We're only having drinks and a takeaway,' Lyndsey said. I could not say to her, My daughter's life will go down the toilet if she does not stop drinking alcohol. I held my tongue. Laura's drinking was a family secret, our pow-wows kept in house. Laura was bemused, the alcohol made her so. Rob and I stormed out. Back home, we told Rachael the sorry tale.

'She's an idiot,' Rob said. 'Let her get on with it. There's nothing more we can do.' Rachael went home.

Later that evening, exhausted by the situation, I felt bad for Laura. The poor girl enjoying an evening with her friend, when her parents disrupted the calm and made a spectacle. Was that not what I wanted for Laura, to entertain good friends? For her to have a good time? So I drove to Laura where I found Lyndsey had gone home and Laura had cleared away the debris of the evening. 'I'm sorry for behaving that way,' I said. 'I'm just so worried about you choosing alcohol to put a smile on your face.' Laura sat on the arm of the settee. She looked away from me. 'Come home?' I offered.

'This is my home,' she said. I hugged her and left.

Back home, I told Rob how desperate I felt. He pulled the duvet over his shoulder. Get to sleep, he implied.

After ten days, I handed Laura her car key. She promised she would never drink and drive again. She was happy to be mobile again after standing at bus stops or walking to work.

I was not aware of what she had missed most of all — illicit meetings with James.

The thank-you she gave

My daughter was like a butterfly. She has them tattooed on her back. She flitted about a lot and was restless staying in one place.

Laura was grocery shopping one day when Rachael bumped into her. She noticed how quickly Laura moved to cover the three bottles of wine in her basket. I told Rob of the three bottles of wine. 'Lots of people drink wine in the evening,' he replied.

'But three bottles?'

'They'll go in that wine-rack.'

I did not agree. 'She never shops for the next day. Those three bottles are for one night. I think she has developed a drinking problem.' We were walking in the fresh clean air. Side by side, taking in the views. He sighed. You see, externally our daughter was managing her life. She went to work, she visited her family, she socialised with friends. Rob thought I should accept that Laura liked a tipple of wine, and not worry about her. But I did.

Laura was no longer James' partner, his live-in lover. She was his mistress. When Laura lived with James, they had arranged for her a car deal for a new black Ford Focus. Rob and I had paid for the trustworthy, smart car that had been exchanged in the deal. Our money disappeared. Without permission, Laura registered her new car to my address. The whisper of the letterbox and a brown envelope hit the mat. I opened the letter: a speeding fine. Laura had travelled at forty-five miles per hour in a thirty-mile zone. The area stated on the fine was near the house of James. Who, according to Laura, she no longer had anything to do with.

I handed the letter to her. She did not mention the ripped envelope. 'Why is your car registered to my address?'

'Just thought it best to do so.'

'No, you didn't. I'm not stupid. You've used this address for a healthy financial check. And why were you speeding near his house?'

'I was going to the shop.'

'What a load of rubbish you do talk.' More lies were fed to me that day. My eyebrows arched when she told me the deal she had signed for on the car, the amount she paid each month.

I always felt sorrow for my daughter living alone. I imagined her with the evenings stretching before her, no one to talk to, no one to share her day. But that's not what she was doing at all; she had a social life we knew nothing about. So much anguish I have wasted on her.

Rob and I invited Laura to join our table of four, a meal at a pub with my sister and her husband. We arrived at Laura's house to collect her. Her car was missing from her parking lot. I telephoned her. 'I'll be there in a minute,' she said. We waited. She zoomed into the courtyard, ten minutes later, and hit the brakes. She slammed her car door and opened the door to ours. Rob's temperature had risen. He turned the key in the ignition and set the car in motion, while Laura fastened the seatbelt. I lectured Laura on careful driving, Rob lectured her on tardiness. Our tutoring complete, silence filled the car. 'I've been to Kelly's. She's having boyfriend trouble. That's why I'm late.'

'You'd know all about that,' I spat. Laura's speech was slow, not slurred. 'Are you all right?' I asked. I swung my head in her direction to look for telltale signs of alcohol consumption.

'I'm tired,' she said. 'I can be tired, for God's sake.'

We joined our dinner guests in the smug warmth of the pub. We scanned the menus, always a trial for Laura. She either wanted a starter as a main course, or something that was not on the menu. The meal was ordered, the wine arrived. After drinking one glass of wine, Laura became drunk. She giggled. 'I don't know what's wrong with me.

Must be because I haven't eaten.' She made repeated trips to the washroom. When she sat at the table, she amused us all with her unique way of viewing life.

I know today what I did not know that evening. I know why she was late and kept Rob and me waiting. She had sped into her parking lot to keep up with her racing heart. She had been with James. That was bad, and this was worse: she had waited for us to leave our house and had entered it secretly to help herself to what she desired.

The thank-you she gave for taking her out. The thank-you she gave for trusting her with our house key. The thank-you she gave for supporting her and loving her. We had no reason to doubt her back then. My house key still belonged to her.

Rob and I were invited to a party we knew we had to attend. Laura was invited too. I offered to collect her. No need for a two-car journey. She clambered onto the back seat and sat quietly. Rob and I shared a look.

New faces at the party introduced themselves as parents of a man we all knew. Laura nodded in recognition and said hello. She asked after their son's welfare. We sat on a sofa, the new people in tow. Then Laura, glass of wine in hand, interrupted the flow of conversation with an absurd question: 'Do you have any children?' Rob and I glared at Laura to prompt her to acknowledge her mistake. Just a short while ago she had asked after their son and now she was asking if they had any children!

All Laura could say was that she was tired and needed rest. Sadness surged in my soul. Her hand by her side, wrapped in a ball, my baby's hand still. I gave a weak smile to our company, and we made our excuse and left.

'You're a bloody disgrace,' Rob said to Laura. 'She's a bloody disgrace,' he said to me. As if in some way we were a pair, my daughter and me. As if in someway I was complicit in her behaviour. We drove away in silence. Laura's head swivelled round. 'I know that lad, driving behind,' she said. Rob and I ignored her. This man drove his car close, he followed our tyre tracks. I pulled the car into her courtyard, the engine still running. We had no reason to stay.

Rob told her to get out. We left Laura standing in the courtyard, searching her bag for keys. Back home, Rob and I stared at the television, with no enthusiasm to watch.

I do not know what Laura did that evening. She may have gone to bed, she may have hooked up with the man who followed us.

Under the influence

I was surprised to see Laura's car charge up the drive. She should have been at work. She rushed into the house. 'I've smashed the window of James' practice.' She caught her breath.

'What do you mean?' Though I knew.

'He wouldn't answer the intercom, and she was inside. I'm not going to be ignored by him.'

James had come out on the street and faced Laura, Sheena behind him. A blazing row broke out amongst all three.

'Laura!'

'Then I drove through the traffic lights on red. I was so mad.'

'Unbelievable! This situation has gotten out of hand.'

Laura was convinced the police would be informed. She was sure I would find out. Why was she under the influence of this destructive man? I grabbed my coat. 'I'm taking you to the doctor; this is ridiculous.'

'Yes, I need help.' She was buzzed with adrenaline. We drove to the surgery in silence. I marched her into the doctor's waiting room. I looked around, no vacant seats.

'I need help with my daughter,' I said to the receptionist. I turned the car keys over and around in my hand. My shallow breathing forced me to take a deep breath. The receptionist led Laura and me to an office to sit and wait. I stared at an empty mug. I wondered what would become of my daughter. I was convinced, and hopeful, the doctor would admit her to hospital. Let a professional put her right, because I could not. I felt as empty as the mug.

We sat side by side, facing our GP. She told the doctor what had happened. 'It's not just that,' I interrupted. 'Her behaviour is spiralling out of control because she drinks too much alcohol.' The taboo phrase had been aired. I had brought the doctor into our secret. The GP looked up from his desk and considered Laura's face. He looked straight into her distressed eyes.

'How much alcohol do you consume?' he asked. A slight tilt to his head.

'A glass, maybe two, in the evening,' she lied.

'What size of glass and where do you fill it to?' I was not invited into their conversation. My daughter was not ready to admit to a drinking habit. I retracted my lips and shook my head. The doctor, who knew us well, looked at me and shrugged his shoulders.

'She drinks more than she is admitting to,' I said. 'And her raging temper, her reluctance to unhinge herself from this awful man, can you give her something to calm her, to make her happy?' The GP wrote out a prescription and handed it to me – Diazepam.

'Only five pills. It is not a long-term solution. Take one if necessary, but,' he looked at me, 'you keep the pills, not her. You give her what she needs.'

Why did he do that? Was Laura at risk of suicide? I did not ask. I did not want to fling this suggestion into my daughter's whirling mind.

Back home, I held the pills in a paper bag. I filled a glass with water, rooted one pill out and handed it to her. I offered her cosy bed to rest in. For an hour I tiptoed around various jobs I had to do. I noticed a tremor in my hand. I looked to my other hand, it did the same. I heard Laura get out of bed. I made my way to the bottom of the stairs. 'How are you feeling?'

'Fine. I'm going home.' She was ready for action again. We both knew she was on her way to James in search of upheaval. I flushed the remaining pills down the toilet.

Diazepam: a class of medicine called benzodiazepines. Helps control feelings of anxiety. Highly addictive.

The mask of alcohol

Before my girls left home I had cooked for four, and now I cooked for only two. But, through habit, the ingredients still amounted to four portions. I put the spare food in plastic containers for the freezer.

I wanted to make sure Laura was eating. One Saturday morning, I packed a stack of these plastic containers filled with frozen delights. I headed off down the street to deliver them to her. I knocked on her door and waited. I knocked again, harder this time: nothing. I rang her telephone number. 'What?' Her tone was flat.

'I'm standing outside your front door.' The phone clicked to silent. I heard her heavy steps come down the stairs. The door opened. I followed her up the stairs to the first-floor landing. A haze of smoke hovered over the living room and the windows were firmly shut. A friend I had not met sat on a settee. 'Hi,' I said, to the friend. 'Laura, what's wrong?'

Laura sat on the opposite settee to her friend, Nikki. She pulled her legs up for comfort. 'I'm just a bit fed up.' A stack of furniture cluttered the room I had decorated. This second-hand furniture belonged to Nikki who sat on the matching settee.

'I don't understand why you feel this way. Clean your house, go for a walk. Come to us for dinner.'

'She's upset over James.' Nikki enlightened me.

'For goodness sake, why are you still bothering with him?'

Nikki sparked up again. 'He comes late at night for, you know … then leaves her in the early hours.'

I looked at my daughter's vacant face. Such hopes I had for this girl. 'Oh, Laura,' was all I could say.

I returned home. Rob and I discussed our daughter's state of mind. 'Should we invite her back home to live?' I asked.

'If that's what you want to do.'

I returned to Laura's house and asked if she would like to come home. And she did. The black plastic bags were packed. I brought Laura home. I emptied a wardrobe for her clothes. Her bedroom embraced her.

The new routine: Laura went to work, came home and had supper with us. Weekends: we went for walks, bought confectionery and watched movies. Laura was looking good. She was happy. Six weeks passed with no problem in sight. How good to have my daughter back home, to have her safe, to feel her happiness and share her laughter.

'I'm going out Saturday night,' she said. My shoulders sank. 'Mum, I can't stay in forever. I need to mix with people my own age. Don't worry, I don't need alcohol to have a good time.' I smiled, my confidence in Laura had grown. Saturday night arrived.

'Don't drink too much and don't be in late,' I said. I prayed.

'I think I'll go to my own house after my night out.'

'Okay.' At least I would not be awake half the night waiting for her to return.

Lunchtime the next day, Laura telephoned. Rob answered, then held the handset out to me, saying, 'She doesn't sound right.'

I took the phone from him. 'Are you okay?' Silence. I put the phone down and headed straight to her house. I knocked on Laura's door: no answer. I dialled her number: voicemail. I knocked again, hard enough to hurt. Laura opened the door. I climbed the stairs behind her. I followed her to the bedroom. She stood by the side of her unmade bed and swayed. 'Are you all right?' Her head bobbed in time with her body, slow and rhythmic. I walked around her bed and picked up a half-drunk bottle of wine. 'This is what's wrong with you. This!' I screamed. I held the wine bottle in the air. I stormed to the bathroom and tipped the wine down the sink. I returned to her side. 'You've been doing so well.' I began to lecture. She flopped on the bed and fell asleep. I did not cover her, I opened the skylight instead. Fury swallowed my anxiety. I snatched her mobile phone from her pillow. There was no resistance from her. I took the phone home to search for traces of James.

Back home, my rage turned to fear. I did not have the courage to search her life online. I held the phone out to Rob. 'I've brought this home, and now I wish I hadn't. I'm going back to post it through her letterbox.' I worried she might need the phone to raise help if she got in a worse state. My anxiety grew, a living, breathing thing which had crept into my body and twisted my organs.

Dusk descended that evening. I nipped out and drove past Laura's house. All windows were lit against the night. This lighthouse was the sign I yearned for. Relief unknotted my organs.

She had company that night. Laura dressed to party some more. I did not know, back then, that cocaine sobered a drunk.

Concerned for her well-being I went to her house the next day. Laura would not open her door, nor answer her phone. I did have a key, but I did not want to use it. I feared what I might find. I went home. Three days dragged by with no contact. My resident anxiety was now a sickness and had taken root for good.

It was evening. Rob was out playing squash, and the phone rang. It was Laura: 'Mum, come and get me.' I dropped everything and ran.

Laura's front door was open. She sat on the stairs, waiting for me, the familiar look of inebriation on her face. She was dressed in dirty pyjamas. I stepped into the hallway. Her hair was greasy, and she was naked of makeup. She sparked up a cigarette, blew smoke in my direction. I did not complain. She had a mug of cold water beside her to accommodate the discarded stubs of nicotine. I looked to the murky water of floating fag-ends. At least she was taking care not to cause a fire. A sprig of comfort I claimed in this hideous situation. 'I'm so unhappy. I don't want to live. I want what Rachael's got. I want my own family.'

'You need help,' I said, feeling helpless.

'No, I don't need help to end it all.' Arrogance had replaced self-pity.

'You can have whatever you want in life. Just stop drinking.'

She looked at me, deep in thought for a nanosecond. She took a deep drag on her cigarette. 'You don't know what it's like being me.'

'No, and you have no idea the pain I go through being your mother.' I stepped outside. The courtyard was lit by welcoming lights. A breeze shifted the leaves on the cultured shrubs. Normality visited for a while. I stepped further away from Laura's front door and telephoned for an ambulance.

I returned to face her, to counsel her, to wait for help to arrive. The ambulance swung round the corner with a police car close behind. Flashing lights, the crackle of radios, the rustle of uniforms alerted Laura. She heaved herself off the stair. 'Have you done this? How could you? I know these people.' She was referring to the paramedics she came in contact with through work.

'Hi, Laura, what's the problem, Love?' asked a paramedic, with a smile.

'Nothing, it's her overreacting.' She pointed a wavering finger in my direction.

A paramedic took my elbow and ushered me aside. 'She's threatening to kill herself,' I said through tears.

He turned to face Laura. 'Do you want to come with me to the hospital? Get yourself checked out?'

'No, there's nothing wrong with me.'

The police assessed the situation, then left. The ambulance crew were about to do the same. 'Please don't.' I begged the paramedic with the welcoming face. 'Please help me with her. She's going to kill herself.'

'No, I am not!' Laura screamed. She fell silent, found her footing and continued. 'I'm not going to hospital.'

'We can't take her against her will,' the paramedic said.

'Then section her,' I said. I knew little about sectioning under the Mental Health Act, other than that my daughter could be taken to hospital against her will. Taken to somewhere safe, with professional care. I was in such turmoil, distress was squeezing all sense out of me.

'No, you don't want to do that, Love. Just take her home with you.'

'I can't. I can't cope. My husband and I have had so much to deal with through her. Please help.'

'Can't, Love. Not going to take her against her will. You take her home.' He turned to Laura. 'Go home with your mum. She'll look after you.'

Laura grabbed a packet of cigarettes, the lighter already clutched in her fist. She slammed the front door. It did not matter that lights were left on in the house. Laura walked by my side to my car. She staggered to the passenger seat, pulled open the door with brute force, then slid down in the seat. The ambulance crew went away, leaving me alone to deal with my daughter. I concentrated on driving. Laura fumbled a cigarette out of the packet and poked it between her lips. 'You're not smoking in my car.' Part of my old-self had kicked in. I had a problem to deal with, I needed to activate my coping mechanism.

Laura and I entered my home. The television played to an empty room. The sound should have been comforting, a living house. Laura went into the kitchen and leant against the cupboard for support. 'I need paracetamol,' she said.

'I don't think that's a good idea in your state.'

'I want paracetamol, the one with codeine.'

I headed to the drawer where medicines were stored. I pulled open the drawer, took out a blister-pack of tablets, and pushed out two. I held them out on the palm of my shaking hand.

'Two! That's no good, I want six.'

'Don't be so stupid.'

'I want six. I know what I am capable of taking.' Laura opened the cutlery drawer to choose a knife.

'What do you think you're doing?'

She closed the drawer, empty handed. She moved toward me. I pushed the medicine drawer shut and stood with my back against it.

'You're not having six.' She looked in my eyes. Her thoughts skipped elsewhere. She chucked the two tablets I offered in her mouth and swallowed them without water. 'Go to bed,' I said.

She placed one foot carefully in front of the other and made her way to the stairs. I steered her into the crisp, clean, marshmallow bed. I pulled the duvet over her and stroked her clammy brow. I went downstairs to say hello to anxiety and wait for Rob to come home.

Laura got out of bed. She stomped around like an imprisoned animal. She called to me, and demanded attention. I ran up the stairs. 'Please be quiet and get back in bed. Dad will be home in a minute. Let me explain what's happened.' She would not go back to bed. Agitation had primed her, she was alert and ready for action. My innards were strangled, like ivy around a vine. I heard Rob's key slide in the lock. He would be expecting a cup of tea and to watch the news. Laura barged past me to accost him.

He took a step back. 'What's going on?' I encouraged him to take a seat. Laura stood beside me, leaning on the door frame for support. I told Rob the sorry tale. He stared into space, his anger fixed his eyes.

'Why won't he look at me?' Laura demanded.

I could feel the heat rise in Rob. I could see he was about to blow. I said to him, 'Please go to Rachael's and stay the night. I'll sort Laura. Please don't make matters worse.'

'I'm not leaving you here with her,' he said. I was frightened that Rob would not be able to contain his anger. I was scared of what the consequence might be. With further persuasion, he went to our married daughter's house. Laura stood and watched at a distance, as if it had nothing to do with her.

After Rob left, Laura became compliant. She went to bed, she went to sleep. I was not fit to invite sleep. I was too restless to watch whatever the television set emitted and switched it off. I boiled water for a cup of tea.

Rachael welcomed her dad into her home. She listened to the horror of our experience. The daughter who was sober, the daughter who carved a life worth living, had concern for me, home alone with the unpredictable Laura. Rachael sent her dad home.

Rob and I shared cups of tea. Exhausted but wide awake, we retired to our bedroom. 'Lock the door,' he said. The lock on our bedroom door was a redundant fixture.

'Why?'

'I don't trust her.'

I slid the lock in place. Rob and I lay in bed and whispered our deep conversation. We were due to go on holiday in two days. Neither of us had the travelling spirit.

Morning's light pushed through a gap in the curtain. I crept into Laura's bedroom. She slept like a baby, my baby still. I gently shook her by the shoulder. 'Wake up. Dad and I will cancel our holiday. We'll go to the doctor, all three of us.' A family engulfed by the same problem.

'Okay.' She rolled over for comfort and slipped back to slumber.

'No, you can get out of bed. We need to discuss your behaviour. We need to sort this out.'

'I'll go to the doctor this afternoon,' she mumbled. She pulled the duvet over her head.

'You can get up now and share what's happening, or you can go home.'

'I'll go home.'

I looked at her cocooned shape and clenched my jaw. I ran downstairs for a roll of black bin liners. Rob followed. 'What's going on?'

'She doesn't want to go to the doctor. She wants to sleep.' Back in Laura's room I stuffed the plastic bags with her belongings. And still she slept. I pulled the duvet off her pyjama body. 'Get up,' I said.

'Why?'

'You want to go home; I'll take you home.'

'What, now?'

'Yep.'

With her alcohol levels depleted, she was submissive. We passed Rob in the hall. Dad and daughter did not speak.

I pushed Laura through her front door and dumped the black bags in the hall. I pulled the door shut behind me. Physically I had dismissed my daughter; mentally she still rode with me.

I came home to breakfast. Rob and I pushed cereal around the bowl in silence. Neither of us had the heart for a holiday. I rang the insurance company. We were not covered for this eventually: our daughter losing her mind.

'That's that, then,' I said to Rob. 'We've lost the money.'

'I think it's drugs,' he said.

'What's drugs? What are you talking about?'

'Laura, she's on drugs.'

'No, no, she's not.' I could not wrap my thoughts around what he had just said. I had no knowledge of drug abuse. I was naive to how widespread drug abuse was. No, not my beautiful daughter, she would not take drugs. She would not even know how to acquire them.

'I'm telling you she is. That behaviour last night did not come out of a bottle of wine. She's on drugs.'

'No, you're wrong. Not drugs,' I said.

He shook his head and looked at me with pity in his eyes. 'What did the insurance company say about the holiday? Have you cancelled?'

'They won't refund the money.'

'Finish packing. We're going.'

We needed this holiday. We took walks in the morning, we sunbathed on the beach and chinked cocktails at sundown before a gourmet meal. Holidays – a break from work and routine. A break from the heartache left at home? No, heartache had a ticket, it followed me. I had left my daughter in a crisis. I looked out to the sea, the sun sinking on the horizon as the moon appeared in full. I listened to the roll of the sea's waves, the cry of gulls. I heard the children's screech of laughter in the distance of the beach. I found in every sight, sound, touch and smell, a memory of my daughter. I was sure I would lose her. I feared she would die.

As I sat on a sun lounger, a text message flashed on my phone from Rachael: Just seen Laura at beauty parlour waiting for a treatment. I was glad, I was mad. Laura had gone from desolation to carefree in a matter of days. This would become a pattern. With each repeat, I suffered in the same way as the first. I could not migrate my thoughts of utter dread. I carried the same fear as if my daughter were a two-year old running out in front of busy traffic.

With our suntan and suitcases, Rob and I headed home. My anxiety climbed at the same height as the aeroplane. I wanted to see Laura, but I dreaded which Laura she would be.

I often visited Laura at her home. I had been shopping with Rachael, and I had a gift of makeup goodies which came with a purchase of perfume. I knew who would enjoy the gift more than me: Laura, my glamorous daughter. I drove to her house with trepidation, schooled to feel this way. I knocked on her door and she opened it. She looked tired, it was late afternoon. 'Not going to ask me in?' I followed her up the stairs. Her kitchen was a tip, the microwave sheltered a stale meal. 'Look at the state,' I said.

'I'll clean it after.'

'After what?'

'Is that why you're here? To have a go at me?'

I ignored the chance of an argument. I held out the gift. A smile embraced her eyes.

'Thanks, Mum. But could you telephone in future? Don't come here unannounced.'

I went home with disappointment as my passenger. And so it was that I would always telephone to herald my arrival. On occasion, I would be told not to come at all.

Pre-arranged, I knocked on Laura's door, she opened it and stepped out. We headed down the street. I had errands she was not interested in. She would meet me in half an hour. She found me in the street, rushed at me with worry planted on her face. 'What's up?' I asked. A resident stone dropped further into my stomach.

'I've just nipped out in my car. A lorry couldn't get past and has damaged the side of my car.'

'Did you get his insurance details?'

'Oh, mm … he was stationary, so I drove past him.'

'Where's your car now?'

'Parked in the courtyard.' We approached her car to inspect the damage. The front pillar was deeply gouged.

'Well, that needs repair,' I said. 'Why did you go out in the car?'

'To get milk.' We had been on the High Street where milk was sold. This bizarre story held no truth. There was no point in interrogating her. I wished I had inspected her car before I knocked on her door.

I took Laura's car to a designated garage for repair. I drove the courtesy car and parked it in the nurse's car park, ready for Laura to collect after her shift. There were many chores I did for Laura. I thought she needed my help. But when my presence was a hindrance to her lifestyle, I was dismissed. But I always came back. I considered it my duty.

Sectioning: Detention under the Mental Health Act. The Mental Health Act is the law which sets out when you can be admitted, detained and treated in hospital against your wishes. This enforced hospital visit is also known as being sectioned. Two doctors must agree that a person is suffering a mental disorder. The patient does have the right to appeal.

Taste of death

Mother's Day, and this was Laura's gift to me: she came early that Sunday morning. A familiar, distant look on her face. 'I need to talk to you,' she said. 'I've run up a bit of debt.' She closed the front door. She confronted her situation head on.

'How much?' Rob asked.

'How come you're in debt? You earn good money,' I asked.

'How much?' Rob's voice had risen above mine.

'Couple of grand,' she muttered.

'A couple of grand!' Rob said.

'A couple of grand exactly, or more than that?' I knew she was feeling her way.

'Well, maybe three thousand.'

'A couple, maybe three! How much do you bloody owe?' Rob demanded.

I jumped in, I wanted to defuse the tension that was building. 'If you want our help, I'll need to see your bank statement.'

Laura shot out of the house to get the statement, and to get away from her dad.

She returned and held out her bank statement. Laura had accumulated a debt of nine thousand pounds. I sat on the bottom step of the stairs. The figures before me shimmied on the paper. Rob took the statement out of my hand, to scan the official list. 'Bloody disgrace,' he said. 'What are you expecting me to do?'

Laura looked to the floor. She did not shrug her shoulders. Rob looked at me, sitting with my head in my hands. 'Right,' he said. 'I'll pay it, but don't ever come to me again to bail you out.'

There were conditions to this gift of money. Laura lost the right to part ownership of her house. Her rent would increase to account for her lack of investment. She would be required to trade in her car for a more modest one. We would arrange a visit to the bank manager and put a stop to this ludicrous overdraft. She accepted all terms, she had no choice. With the bank statement in her fist, she closed the front door behind her. She left us reeling.

'Drugs,' Rob said. We watched Laura's car pull off the drive. 'I'm telling you, it's drugs. You don't go through that sort of money buying wine.'

'It's not drugs.' I was adamant. I was aware people took drugs, hardened people who lurked in alleyways in the dark of night. People whose bed was a cardboard box. No, my daughter abused alcohol, she did not take drugs. She was not one of 'those' people. I did not know how prevalent drug-taking was in a town like ours, a vibrant, healthy town.

It did not bother Laura, nor did it bother me, what the bank manager thought of a twenty-seven-year-old professional woman bringing her mother to an appointment to discuss her own debt.

Laura and I sat in the wood-clad room of the bank manager's office. He pushed back in his spring-backed chair, laced his fingers together and waited for Laura to begin. It was me who spoke first, it was me that had things to say. 'How come she has been allowed to run up so much debt?'

'Laura has sufficient funds deposited each month, her debt is manageable.'

'Manageable for the interest charged,' I said. I handed over a cheque, made out to the sum of nine thousand pounds. 'You can take this overdraft, this availability of funds, off her account.'

He leant forward with my cheque in his hand. Laura looked at the desk which separated her and me from him. I gave a half-smile as she stared at literature for savings accounts.

'What say we reduce the overdraft to two thousand pounds?'

'No overdraft,' I said.

'What about food, Mrs Sefton? What if it's the end of the month and her salary hasn't cleared?'

'Food? She's not spending this sort of money on food.' I had disclosed more than I intended.

Laura had been dangled a two-thousand-pound spending spree. That was all she could hear, that was all she could see.

91

Her account, her choice, a two-thousand-pound overdraft was in place. Her eyes sparkled as she considered this available fund.

I knew we had not found a resolution to Laura's wayward spending. It occurred to me that I might buy one too many pairs of shoes, but I had Rob to reign me in. Laura did not share her bank account, and her spending went unchecked. I offered to help manage her finances. Good idea, she agreed. She handed over her bank statement and cash card. I discovered a spending pattern on a night out: several withdrawals of ten pounds. 'Why?' I asked.

'I take out what I need, when I need it.'

My main concern was her welfare. 'I don't like you popping out of pubs and clubs, crossing busy roads and standing at a cash machine when you've been drinking.'

'Don't worry about that. I gave my card to a friend to draw the money out.' Not one alarm went off in her head. We argued. 'It's none of your business what I do with my card, or what I spend money on. Give me my card back. I'll manage my own money.'

'Fine.' I thrust the card onto her open hand. 'Don't come crying to me when your finances don't stack up.'

Usually, Laura liked to connect, she would telephone me at least once a day, get the job out of the way before she started drinking. Friday, no telephone call. Saturday, no telephone call. Sunday morning, not one word from her. The calls I made to her phone went straight to voicemail. 'What if she's dead in her bed?' I said. This scenario had been touring my mind all weekend.

Rob, who is not swamped with unwanted emotions, allowed the colour to seep from his face. 'We'll go and have a look.' We got in the car like we were attending a funeral. We parked our car in Laura's space on the courtyard. Tension connected Rob to me as we opened her front door. On wooden legs we climbed the first flight of stairs. The living room was tidy, the kitchen was empty. We took the second flight of stairs with caution in each move. I opened her bedroom door. The room was tidy, the bed made. We checked the spare room and the bathroom. And breathe again we did. We drove to her place of work, but her car was not in the car park. We drove past the street where James resided; her car was not there.

Back home I tried to ignore the fear clutching at my throat. Rob ate his Sunday dinner, I scraped mine into the bin. Rob was tired of the images I projected of our daughter's well-being. He watched a football match on the television, coaching the players and shouting at the referee. The telephone rang. I picked up the receiver and held it to my ear. 'Hi, Mum,' Laura said.

'Where've you been?' I shouted. Rob looked up from the game.

'What's your problem? I've been out with friends.'

'Why didn't you ring and tell me? You always ring.'

'For God's sake, I'm not a child. I don't have to check in with you.'

'No, but you always do, so when you don't … well, Dad and I have been worried sick.' Rob returned his attention to the match. Laura would not accept my logic of concern. She would not say sorry.

This is what happened on that lost weekend, when I had tasted the image of death: Laura was with a new man. The sort of man who would catch James' attention. Peter had the looks, the career, the money. He was kind and thoughtful. He had interests Laura might enjoy. Oh, and he had a girlfriend. On this lost weekend, he had taken Laura away to a smart hotel. Why could she not have told me this? Maybe there had been a drama. Maybe there had been a show.

Peter wanted a secret liaison with Laura, hidden from his girlfriend.

He wanted to see how this relationship with Laura developed. Laura wanted to parade Peter to catch James' eye. Peter came to Laura's house for a couple of months, he doted on her. Said his girlfriend was a wreck, and worried about the consequences of leaving her. Laura did not mind. Fine by her that Peter was committed elsewhere, he had done his job. James came back to her. She ended the relationship with Peter and gave me the gifts he had presented her with. She did not tell me the reason why she no longer met with Peter.

A sunny Sunday, armed with Rob, I knocked on Laura's door. 'Would you like to spend the day with us, and come for a walk?' I held the beloved white terrier on a lead; Rachael was on holiday.

'No thanks.' We stood in the courtyard. Laura stroked the dog.

'It's a beautiful day, come with us,' I said.

'I can't. I'm waiting for someone.'

'Someone?'

Laura paused. I could see the lies jump behind her eyes.

'It's not that arsehole is it?' I was referring to James. Silence told me what I wanted to know.

'Come on,' Rob said. He took the lead off me and led the dog away.

On this gorgeous day our daughter chose to sit on her step and wait for that awful man to visit. We all knew he would be late. We all knew he was in the bookies. He gambled every day. When he lost money he would be vile. When he won money he would shove a handful of clean notes into my daughter's grabbing hand. He gambled everything: he gambled my daughter's future, he gambled her sanity. Rob was the grandson of an illegal bookmaker, way back when. 'There's only one winner – the bookie,' he would say.

So, James was still prominent in my daughter's life. Some of the things she told me when it did not matter anymore: they met in car parks, the illicit lovers. He took her to restaurants, he courted her all over again. Sheena lived with him and Laura was his concubine. A naughty thing they shared, a naughty thing they enjoyed.

James owned cars that would draw the attention of anyone's eye. He took Laura to view a mansion he reckoned he would buy. As they drove away from the property, Rob chugged past in his van in the opposite direction. Sitting in the passenger seat of the poser's car, Laura saw her dad and held a magazine in front of her face to hide from him; the dad who loved her so.

James was jealous of Laura's family life and the love we shared. He demanded Laura make his presence known. He wanted her family to suffer, he wanted to show how powerful he was in her life. But Laura was reluctant. She knew we did not approve.

A short time after, Rob and I were busy gardening. We had not heard from Laura all weekend: now a regular event. The telephone rang. I ripped off a gardening glove and answered. 'Can I come and see you, with Nikki?' Laura asked. 'To tell you what's been going on.'

I put the phone down and took a moment to steady myself, then went back outside to Rob.

'Laura's coming to see us.'

'What now?'

Nikki drove onto our drive; the passenger door opened and Laura got out, dressed in pyjamas. She was stick thin and fatigued. Manners forced me to offer coffee to Nikki, while my heart bled and I could have fallen on my knees to beg for Laura to be her former self.

Into the conservatory Laura and Nikki went. I followed. Rob put in an appearance, soiled gardening gloves still on his hands. 'What's the problem?' He asked. He looked directly at Laura and ignored Nikki, the friend he had not met.

'It's, just, I've come with Nikki to tell you what's been happening to me.'

'And what's that then?' Irritation masked his fear.

'I've been drinking.'

Rob said no more. He went back to the garden. He carried on digging what he understood: the earth. He did not have the skill to excavate the mind of his daughter.

I hung on Laura's every word. 'Stop drinking,' I said. As if it was as simple as that.

Nikki joined in, her purpose in coming. 'I keep telling Laura, she should tell you the truth.'

'What's that then, the truth?'

Laura chimed in. 'It's about my drinking, that's all.' She glared at Nikki. Laura stood. I hugged her. I could feel her skinny frame through the thinness of her pyjamas. Too tight a squeeze and she would have disintegrated in my arms.

'Please stop drinking,' I whispered in her ear.

Many years later we have the facts, the state our daughter was in the day she came to visit with Nikki, the day Rob and I gardened. It was not really about drinking at all – it was about drugs. James had supplied Laura with drugs, then summoned Nikki to take care of the state Laura was in, because he would not. As Rob had said, our daughter was abusing drugs.

It made no difference in my mind whether we knew the facts about her drug use back then. I had been introduced to her eating disorder. I knew about her alcohol consumption. There was nothing I could do. How could I compete with illegal drugs? What could I offer? A cup of tea, a slice of toast, a mother's love? My daughter was lost to me more than I realised.

A constant bereavement

We had our good days, we shared good times. Our daughter returned to happiness. This is hard for a parent of an addicted child. The problem child functions, carries on with a successful career, has good times socially. We think there is no longer a problem, we hope and pray. Events happen, events are put right. Then, out of nowhere, it all falls apart. Feelings of utter despair, of looking at the night sky wondering if your child roams the street or is comatose in bed. A siren bleats and panic sets in. Is the ambulance heading for your loved one? You walk the street with a smile on your face and broken glass in your heart. You see your child's peers progressing, and wonder why your child cannot enjoy life in the same manner. A house with a curtain closed in the midday sun conjured an image of my daughter ill in bed. Music in the distance, drifting in the air, would she hear it too? I wanted to see Laura, I needed to see her. But the thought of bumping into her frightened me. I dreaded an alcoholic usurping my daughter's beautiful face. Then the child I fear, the addict, appears at my door, her cheeks a healthy glow. Dressed in uniform, her lipstick bright and cheery. She gives me freesia, a bunch of sweet-smelling colour. She shares her wit, her plans, and dreams for the future. And I relax. But the cycle starts again: the cycle of a constant bereavement.

This was the state my mind was in when Laura arrived at my door and held out her defunct engagement ring from the wedding that never was. She wanted to socialise, but she had no money. 'I can pawn this for forty quid. Do you want to give me more?' She asked.

'You should keep it,' I said.

'I don't want it. It's going one way or another. Can you give more for it?'

'If you want me to have your cast-off engagement ring, I would have thought you'd give it to me.'

'So, that's a no?'

I was speechless. Laura went to the pawn shop to get forty pounds for a ring worth more than that. I made a cup of tea and waited for Rob to come home, to tell him how thoughtless our daughter had become.

Laura did not return to the pawn shop to collect the engagement ring she pawned, she did not have forty pounds to spare. She owned a gold coin, a christening present. She asked Rob to buy it for a fiver. 'Yeah, I'll have it,' Rob said. It had come to this: rummaging in her belongings to scrounge for money. She used to be kind, she used to be generous. Her need to escape through the door that alcohol and drugs held open robbed her of these qualities.

The aroma of an alcoholic

Great joy, the whole family is blessed, Rachael had given birth to a gorgeous baby boy. Laura was to be his godmother. Our new baby endowed with the face of an angel, swaddled in his christening shawl.

The night before the christening, Laura said she would relax in a bubble bath, and paint her nails red. We assembled in the church. I looked over to Laura. The cream suit she wore hung on her like clothes on a hanger. Her nails were chipped pink, her hair was slick with product. Make-up could not hide the dark circles under her eyes. The girl who spent hours in front of a mirror perfecting the look she desired, the girl who stood before Rob and me, pleased with the compliments she received … where had she gone?

The church service over, we amassed in the pub where a buffet was laid out for guests. Two hours were chatted by. Laura came and sat by my side. Her eyes had lost mobility, her speech was erratic. I pretended not to notice. A crowd of men, friends of the baby's father, decided to take their party away from the family environment. Laura tagged along, following the men through the door. The next day I learnt how Laura had drunk herself paralytic with these men. Someone always had a tale to tell, with no consideration of how distressed the tale made me feel.

I sat at my desk, punching data into the computer. The telephone rang. It was Laura: 'Mum, I've been caught drink-driving.'

I hid my despair behind a lecture: 'Well, you ignored all warnings.'

Rob was at work, and it would be late when he got home. On top of all the hassle thrown his way, this news would be one more stress to burden him. I practised the speech I had planned for him. I would prepare his meal, wait for him to take a shower, then tell him. I could not concentrate on what I was doing. I wandered to the window, sat back down on the settee. Rob's van reversed up the drive. I told Rob as soon as he walked in the house, I could not contain my apprehension. His expression was not of anger or sadness, but of resignation. That it had come to this.

This was the first issue our daughter would have to deal with on her own. The law held the power now, not us. I would not attend court with her. I would not support what she had done. A casual boyfriend accompanied her. It was 2005. Laura received a twelve-month driving ban and a fine. She told me later she had demanded that this casual boyfriend take her to a pub where she got bladdered. Laura then went on a two-week bender.

The short spell of being a pedestrian I had enforced on her was now permanent. 'I'm glad I've lost my licence,' she said. 'Now I can drink what I like and not worry about driving.' She said the police had been good to her, even chatted for a while. What had my daughter developed into? The little girl who got out of bed and stood at the top of the stairs to confess a minor misdemeanour had gone.

The day of my fiftieth birthday, my daughters and I would go shopping, our new baby too. Rachael drove to Laura's with the baby strapped in the back of her car. All three came to my house and gave me a bunch of flowers.

Laura sat in the front seat next to Rachael. I sat in the back with my darling grandson. Our customary birthday treat was a trip to the shopping centre. We were bobbing along the road, dance tunes played in the car, when Laura chirped up. 'I was locked in a cell when I was picked up for drink-driving.'

'I don't want to hear this,' I said.

'The policeman flirted with me,' Laura laughed.

'Laura! Mum doesn't want to know. Shut up.'

We arrived at the shopping centre and strapped the baby in his buggy. I planted a kiss on his precious nose. We headed for a shopping experience. We picked up this, we put back that. The lights were bright, the atmosphere invigorating. Rachael tried on a pair of shoes. Laura and I sat close to each other on a leather cube. I could smell alcohol leaking from her pores. A smell I was familiar with: the aroma of an alcoholic. 'You stink of alcohol,' I said. 'Have you been drinking this morning?'

'No.'

I gave a lecture on alcohol consumption which she chose to ignore. Rachael joined the queue to pay for the shoes. Laura took a chance, she had my ear. 'Mum, I'm in debt. I've no money.'

'Why are you telling me?' She shrugged her shoulders. A sulk clamped onto her face. Another stone dropped in my stomach, adding to the rubble.

Rachael put the fancy pink carrier bag of shoes on the arm of the baby's buggy, adding to her previous purchases. How different my two girls had become. We coveted sunglasses set out in a glass case. Laura saw a pair she liked, she smiled at me for permission. I bought the sunglasses to make her happy, I bought them to ease the sickness in my heart. It was my special day and she had ruined it.

Six months later we had a family event: a nephew was getting engaged. He held a party at his apartment with his fiancee by his side. All family members were invited. Rob and I collected Laura and told her to behave. We parked the car and walked to my nephew's apartment. We carried gifts to his door. I walked behind Laura. She was wearing a fur coat and high-heeled shoes. I couldn't help noticing how skinny her legs had become. She had sores on her ankles from wearing too tight ankle straps.

Laura had gone on a date the previous evening with a suitable prospect. I asked how the date went.

'I don't think I'll be seeing him again.'

We greeted and kissed the nephew and his fiancee. We accepted drinks, wine for Laura. I shot her a look, one she was familiar with: moderate your alcohol intake. We sat in the room and mingled with different guests. My father, with strong opinions on how one should behave, sat opposite Laura. Her fur coat still on her back, her head bent over her mobile phone, busy texting, she had the odd chuckle to herself. Father shot me a look, one that I was familiar with: chastise your daughter for her ignorance. He expected me to take the phone off Laura as if she were a two-year old.

Laura told me, much later, the person texting was the man from the night before. The reason why the date had not gone well? Laura was drunk when he collected her. She fell asleep in the pub. When he woke her, she snarled at him and demanded to be taken home.

We left the engagement party and made our way home. Laura made a phone call. With no choice, I listened. She made an arrangement with someone to meet outside a club.

'Who's that then?' I asked.

'A friend.' We neared the nightclub which was down an unlit road. 'Can you drop me off here at the corner?'

'No, we'll take you to the entrance,' I said.

'I'm meeting my friend here on the corner.'

Rob pulled the car to an abrupt stop. I used to ferry my daughter wherever she wanted to go, no standing on street corners for her. I did not want to leave her here alone on this dark and shadowy street. I protested.

'For God's sake, I am not a child,' she complained.

Rob shook his head at me, a remark in his eyes. She got out of the car. I watched her through the car's side window as we drove away. She was busy on her mobile phone. 'We should have taken her to the door,' I said.

'Why? She'd only walk to the corner, and you'd be none the wiser.'

A few weeks had passed by when Rachael paid Rob and me a visit. 'I've just been to see Laura. I'm worried about her. Can she come home and live with you?' We were reluctant to offer our home to Laura again. But, we loved her, we worried about her, we needed to support her. I drove to Laura's house to ask her to come home.

'Can I, really?'

'Grab a few things, we can come back for the rest.' The black bin liners could wait. Laura's mobile phone vibrated a tune. She answered: A friend of James. I snatched the phone out of her hand, took the back off the phone and broke the SIM card. She did not kick up a fuss; she wanted to come home with me.

The next day, Laura and I went to the phone shop to purchase a new SIM card. Back home, she passed the new number to family and friends. When I was out of the room, she texted the number to James. I have no idea how many mobile numbers she has had, I lost count at ten.

We had a routine for a while. Laura stayed with Dad and me during the week, then went to her house at the weekend.

All was good. Gradually she moved back to her house, saying she wanted the responsibility of being alone. The auburn shampoo I bought for her sat by the side of the bath.

Laura showed me her payslip, the money she had earned for the hours she put in. I smiled, a welcome change from the debt she was in. The day after, I checked my bank balance for her rent to have been paid but there was nothing. That familiar sick feeling scraped the lining of my stomach. I did not mention the debt to Rob for a couple of days. I just checked the account. Where in figures the rent money should have been was a big fat zero. A foreboding jumped into my mind. It was time to confess to Rob. He stopped what he was doing. 'She's not taking the piss out of me,' he declared. He took his mobile phone out of his utility trouser pocket. 'Why haven't you paid your rent?'

'Sorry, I haven't got the money.'

'She hasn't got it,' Rob said to me. 'Un-bloody-believable.' Back to Laura's ear his speech went. 'You can find somewhere else to live. You're not living rent free off me.' End of conversation. Telephone back in his pocket. He picked up a screwdriver and applied force to a screw. I hovered behind him.

'She showed me how much she had earned the other day,' I said.

'And I'm telling you it's drugs, that's where her money is going.' I did not challenge him, I knew better. 'You're not talking me out of this. She will leave that house. I'm not funding her lifestyle.' I swallowed my tears. A lovely house for my lovely daughter. Why did she not value what we had done for her? Where would she go? This was a new worry to stack on top of the old.

I spoke with Rob. 'She's only missed one payment.'

He was adamant. 'She can sling her hook.'

Laura resigned herself to leaving, telling us Nikki thought the house we provided was a depressing place. Nikki who had dumped her furniture to turn Laura's living space into a fire salvage shop. Nikki rented a one-bedroom flat, there was one available for rent in the block. Laura did not have the money for a deposit or the rent in advance. Rob and I paid it. He wanted her out of the modern, light and airy, three-storey house she found depressing. The inferior place Laura chose to rent cost the same amount of money we had charged. She packed her black bin liners. She left coat hangers to swing in the fitted wardrobes. I took her redundant car and parked it outside her new address.

Laura and I arrived at the flat, the one she had told me was nice. I walked through the shared front door. An internal door to the right had a lock on it. Laura opened this door with a key. We stepped into the dingy living room, where a free-standing wardrobe lent against a wall. The kitchen was compact and modern. To the side of the kitchen was a shower and toilet. Sitting in the bedroom was the boiler for hot water, with little room for anything else. I tried to remain positive, to be upbeat. 'The kitchen's lovely,' I managed to say, though the kitchen had no window.

'It's a fresh start,' Laura said. 'It's time I stood on my own two feet.' We both knew she did not mean what she said. I could have cried for her. I did not, but the sick feeling tumbled in my stomach.

Rob paid Laura a visit to see where his daughter now lived. He chastised her for having only one working light bulb. He went to the electrical supplier to purchase a box of lightbulbs because he loved her so.

105

Laura now admitted she had a problem with alcohol. The doctor recommended a twelve-step support group.

One evening Rob and I drove past a bus stop where Laura stood. We knew where she was going: her first meeting of support. My beautiful daughter waited to meet people who shared the same issue as her. The knot tightened in my stomach as I hoped to catch a wave from her. She should have been going home to a family, her own. She should have been going to work, or out on a date. Not going to a meeting with alcoholics, like her. Afterwards, she said the meeting was therapeutic and that she would attend more.

I asked Laura to dinner one evening. She declined, an alcohol meeting to attend. The meetings appeared to be of use, to do her good. She had been encouraged to make peace with herself and love her own spirit. I relaxed to the concept. Rob arrived home late from work. 'Have you heard from Laura today?'

'Yes, she's gone to a meeting.'

'Really? I've just seen her. I wouldn't think they hold meetings outside a pub.' She had lied to me again.

Laura was to call at my house the next day to share lunch before going to work. The telephone rang at lunchtime. 'I won't be coming. I don't have time. I need to nip into town before work.'

'Are you okay?' I asked.

'Yes, too much to do, that's all,' she drawled.

I jumped in the car and drove to her flat. I knocked on her door with vigour. She opened the door, allowed me to follow her inside. She was wearing pyjamas, she was drunk. She hunkered down on the settee. 'I'm sorry, Mum.'

'Oh, Laura, why?' I looked around the untidy, miserable flat. 'Come home. Let me look after you.'

With reluctance, she clambered into my car. I took her home. I got a pillow and duvet and made a bed on the settee. I switched on the television and found a programme she would enjoy. I turned down the volume. I closed the sitting-room door and left her in peace. A couple of hours shuffled by. I went to check on her. Alcohol seeped out of her skin and filled the room with its stale stench. I made her a cup of coffee. I had nothing to say.

Rob came home from work. 'What's she doing here in that state?' I ushered him to the kitchen. I pacified him. I said I was worried about her state of health. His two eyebrows became one. 'She's not staying. She's not coming here to live.'

'I know.' And I did. It was pointless trying to mother her, trying to keep her sane. I made Laura something light to eat. She asked to take a bath. I found clean clothes of mine for her. We could hear the noise of running water through the tightly closed door. Laura reappeared, refreshed.

'Why have you got in this state? I thought you were meant to be in work.' Rob could hold his tongue no longer.

'Don't start,' Laura said.

'That's it, you can go.' Rob put his shoes on and ushered Laura out of the door. With a bag of groceries I had pulled together, he drove her home.

Laura continued with the twelve-step programme. She learnt that she did not drink casually but deliberately. The support group did not stop her from drinking. She would sit with others and share tales of abuse. The hurt she had caused her loved ones. The desperate times she had encountered. All addicts are self-centred. Laura would listen to the tales of members. She would consider her behaviour to be not as bad. She had room for manoeuvre. She picked up tips for fooling people. She shared tips of her own. In fairness, Laura had met some good and kind people through the twelve-step programme. Professional people who had lost so much. Laura belonged to this group, and I was thankful that she found others clambering onto the raft. She learnt that the idea that someday she would be able to have one drink and be in control was fiction. There was no such thing as making a normal drinker out of an alcoholic. The twelve-step programme, in my opinion, did not save Laura. The steps were rigid. She would be assigned a mentor. She would achieve several steps, stumble into the arms of alcohol, and be forced to return to step one. Each time she tripped, she crawled back to the beginning. It became cyclic, attending meetings, then drinking. Back to one, two, then three steps. An alcoholic thrives on repetition, it is what they know, what they are comforted by.

The twelve-step programme was introduced in 1939 and has stuck to the same format ever since. The programme has made no allowance for cultural change. Though the programme has helped some. And so my daughter found another cycle. Like a hamster on a wheel, she used the twelve-step programme to seek refuge and company, not to reform.

A tale came my way, the same carrier pigeon as before. Laura had dined in a restaurant in the company of friends. She stepped out of the restaurant, intoxicated. Opposite was a lively drinkers' pub. An older man, Fred, a heavy-drinking man with failed marriages behind him, saw Laura standing on the pavement. He downed his drink. In his worn trainers, t-shirt and jeans he crossed the road. He asked Laura to join him. And she did. She carried on drinking, then went home with this boozer of a man. A gaggle of nodding heads could not believe Laura had hooked up with one such as he. My quick-witted daughter was amused by his jokes: 'I used to own a paper shop but it blew away'. Hearing her, was like listening to a stranger. Laura's development had stalled. She no longer acquired new knowledge. She had halted her experience. Her thoughts and humour had stagnated. The imagination she owned to forge her wit had gone to sleep, had passed out through alcohol; how that broke my heart.

Laura moved in with Fred, her drinking buddy. He provided alcohol to flow at his expense.

Laura would often agree to come home for Sunday dinner, and just as often would not show. I walked to the newsagent on a sunny Sunday morning, bought a newspaper for me and a magazine for her. I sauntered home with the reading material stashed under my arm. Rob was working. Back home, I placed two deck chairs in a sunny spot. Out of the freezer I took Laura's favourite chicken kebab. I ignored Rob's advice not to get anything out for her dinner because she wouldn't come.

I waited for Laura to wander up the drive. Morning met afternoon, the telephone rang. 'Mum, I'm not coming. I'm going to sit in my friend's garden instead.' I slammed the phone down. All I asked was that she stick to her arrangement. I sat for a minute and looked at the telephone nestled in my hand. I redialled her number. A man's voice answered. 'Hello, Love,' he said. I could hear the grin on his face. I slammed the phone down for a second time.

The next day, Laura appeared at my door. She held a cellophane-wrapped bouquet of flowers. She offered the flowers to me. 'I'm sorry, Mum.' I snatched the flowers off her, stormed to the back of the house, and rammed them in the bin.

'Now piss off,' I said. I did not want gifts. I wanted her. I wanted her to be sober. I wanted her to be the girl she used to be: a daughter to me.

Here is a tale from her own mouth: one sunny afternoon outside a pub, she and Fred were so drunk that they fell asleep on the cobbles. I could have walked past them, a grandson in each hand. Two grandsons, Rachael had blessed us with at this time. The landlord woke Fred and Laura and asked the pair to move on. How proud that made me feel!

The relationship with Fred became explosive, fuelled by the octane of alcohol. Laura flirted with other men in front of Fred; he left the pub and went home. Later that night Laura knocked on his door, he would not let her in. Sometime later, Laura told Rachael that she had slept on a park bench that night. Incapable of making her way to her flat. She came from Park Lane, and accepted park bench.

Nikki, who was now Laura's neighbour, cleaned premises for a living. Laura was seen cleaning offices at a quarter to seven one morning. Laura's reward: a bottle of wine. 'What are you playing at when you can't attend your own commitments?' I demanded. Laura denied the casual labour.

Laura was now officially on long-term sick leave from her role as a nurse. Weeks became months and still Laura had not returned to work. There was to be a meeting with her employer to discuss the situation. Nikki went with her. Laura confided in staff members the problems she was having with self-medication. The mess she had made of her life. Laura informed the people assembled that she intended to seek treatment to put her life back together. The management offered Laura a sabbatical: a year off without pay. Laura was given a week to consider the offer.

'Surely they can't do that, lay you off?' I asked. 'You have a sick-note.'

'It's either a year out, or I'll be sacked.'

I attended the follow-up meeting with Laura, as did a union representative. A desk separated two people facing Laura and me, and another two people sat at each end. Out of the window the green hills could be viewed. It was agreed that Laura would take the year out. A tear tumbled onto my cheek, followed by others. I could see the sorrow on the faces of people I did not know.

Laura and I left the meeting. She marched to her ward to collect her payslip. I followed in her wake, a handkerchief clutched in my fist. From a wire tray, Laura took her payslip. She ripped the envelope open and scanned the slip of paper while her mind headed to the off-licence. She looked at me and said, 'What are you crying for?' That was all she had to say.

All the studying she had completed, the support we had given, the train journeys and car rides, the joy she found caring for patients, had gone, slipped through her fingers like red liquid poured from a bottle.

Laura became tired of treading the path she had chosen, tired of where life had taken her. As she told her manager, she wanted to seek treatment, she wanted to go to rehab. Or was she was running away from responsibility, her debt? Laura contacted the authorities and gained access to the support she needed. With a person in authority, Laura visited a rehabilitation centre and was offered the next available place. I took her decision in my stride. I did not know what else to do.

I organised Sunday dinner the day before Laura was admitted for treatment. She would stay at a detox centre for two weeks before transferring to a rehabilitation centre for twelve months. Rachael and her family attended this meal, a farewell gathering. We sat around the dinner table and chatted, like a normal event. I could not swallow my food. My head was a sackful of pain. My lips smiled at the conversation and I nodded when appropriate. But then I just couldn't take it anymore so I excused myself from the table, kissed Laura's cheek and wished her well, and took myself to bed.

Laura told me recently, 'I stole two bottles of wine before leaving your house that Sunday. I slid a bottle into each slipper you bought me for rehab.'

Little girl lost

The next day, Laura waited by a lamppost at the top of her street, early morning, for a member of the care team to collect her. I knew this was happening. I pictured my beautiful, lonely daughter waiting for a stranger to take care of her. Like the stranger who fed her as a baby, when I could not. I poured my love to her in a text message.

Laura had given me the key to her flat. She asked if Rob and I would collect her belongings, get rid of the furniture we could not store and hand the key back to the agent. Rob and I entered the dismal flat. As much as I hated this place, I hated it more now that my darling daughter was no longer present. We took her furniture to the refuse tip and picked up her plastic bags. Her whole life, and what she had achieved, was contained in those bulging black sacks. I took one last look around the place to make sure we had everything. The mirror Laura and I had shopped for still hung on the wall.

Mirror, mirror on the wall, what have you seen? No doting husband reflected there, or laughing children brushing their hair. Instead, you gave reflection to an alcoholic woman, steadying her hand to apply lipstick. I took the mirror home and stashed it in the loft, to collect dust, not memories.

The detox centre: Laura needed medication and guidance to come off alcohol before she could attend rehab. The medication of choice was Librium, also known as chlordiazepoxide, which acts on the brain and nerves to produce a calming effect. Laura was given a reducing dose to stop dependency on the drug developing. Librium is used in place of alcohol because if an alcoholic stops drinking abruptly they are at risk of having a seizure. She had completed one week of her two-week stay. I received a phone call. 'Mum, can you and Dad come and visit to meet my care worker?'

Christmas Eve was the day we went to visit Laura at the detox centre. Rob and I dreaded the idea of seeing our daughter there. We arrived at the huge Victorian house on a tree-lined street. Men in hooded jackets milled outside the grand entrance, dragging on cigarettes. We walked through the huddled haze of smoke and entered the premises. Rob took a deep breath of unwanted nicotine. Not wanting to look at the men, his attention was caught by a plaque on the wall: Mental Health Services. This connotation hit him hard. We stepped into the hall. The stench of institutionalised food smacked my senses. The lights were bright, interrogating, no corners to take privacy in. We walked past the dayroom where hardened men sat. I was aware that colour had seeped from my face. Rob stared ahead. We were greeted by a care worker and led down a corridor where bedroom doors were locked. In a private room, our daughter sat with her care worker.

This care worker was younger than our daughter. What experience could this girl have? She introduced herself. She did not offer her hand for either one of us to shake. I looked at Laura and smiled. She looked good, the best she had in a long time. The care worker spoke about forgiveness and how important it was that we forgive Laura. We, the loving parents who had supported our daughter the best we were able, when the same daughter treated us badly, were lectured on forgiveness. The care worker said, 'In my experience, Laura will be one of the ones to make it.'

'Make what?'

'To recover, to become clean.' Rob and I listened, we wanted to believe. Laura watched for our reaction. She was pleased with the recommendation she had been given. 'So, Laura, you said you would confess to your mum and dad?'

Confess what? I looked from the care worker to Laura.

'Well,' Laura said, 'the thing is…'

'The thing is what?' I pushed her along.

'It's not just alcohol I have been abusing. I have been taking cocaine.'

'Okay,' I said.

'I told you,' Rob said, looking at me.

Laura took the stage. 'But you don't need to worry. I only do cocaine when I have been drinking, and I won't be drinking again.'

'Well, that's reassuring,' I said.

'And the other thing I want to tell you …,' Laura continued.

'The other thing!' I screeched.

'I've been stealing from you. Bottles of wine.'

I relaxed, I knew this, and the rest of what she stole. I looked at Laura. None of what she said mattered. Rob and I knew her situation to be serious. 'That's all in the past; get yourself well and we can start over,' I said. I wanted her to believe life could be normal once more. I wanted to believe this too.

The meeting was over. Laura took us to the dining room, explaining that all meals were cooked for the residents. At a table, a young lad sat facing his parents, he lifted his hand in recognition of Laura. I shared with his parents a smile of awareness. They looked like decent people. They were of a similar age to Rob and me. Relief swept over me. We were not the only ones to have lost a child to addiction. Not the only parents to think we had done wrong. We said goodbye to Laura. We shared hugs and kisses.

Rob and I went to Rachael's house from the detox centre. We went to share Christmas Eve. We had a meal. I delighted in my grandsons' excitement. Rob was quiet. Usually, he was happy in this environment, usually he made it whole. We went home to bed.

Christmas Day we awoke to a lack of joy. I cancelled our planned visits. Rob could not contain his grief. Our problem child was sick: her alcohol addiction more powerful than she.

'We've abandoned her to a place full of hardened addicts. All of them men,' he sobbed.

I was accustomed to feelings of utter despair regarding Laura. Rob's work took his energy and his mind away from his daughter, and left little room for emotion. Today he had time to reflect. We sat on the settee with mugs of tea. We spoke to Laura on the telephone, she sat at the payphone in the corridor of the detox place, and heard her dad sobbing on the other end of the line. The conversation did not elevate our unhappy state.

A charity had sent Christmas presents to the detox centre. Laura opened a wrapping of bubble bath and slippers. It warmed my heart: the kindness of strangers.

The two weeks of detox had been completed. Laura was transported to the rehabilitation centre. More strangers to take care of her.

Cocaine with ecstasy

Recently, I learnt more about what had been going on. Laura and I sat opposite each other at her kitchen table one day. The back door was open, and invited sunshine into the room.

Me: 'When did you start doing drugs?'

Laura: 'I was introduced to drugs by James. I wanted to take it. I had been drinking and he produced a line of coke. I snorted it. I enjoyed the feeling, the buzz from the drug, it gave me confidence. Cocaine sobered me.'

Laura went on to tell me of her weekend stays in posh hotels with James: 'We took cocaine, and added to the buzz by swallowing ecstasy tablets.'

Behaviour I did not want to hear was disclosed to me. I had to listen for the sake of her story. At a nightclub, James said he needed the toilet. He hid behind a wall to watch Laura. A man chatted to her, not unusual for her attractiveness. James, aroused by jealousy, dragged Laura out of the club by her hair. In the hotel bedroom, he jumped on her and rubbed the makeup from her face. Telling her to look at herself in the mirror: 'See what you look like now, you ugly bitch!'

116

Laura locked herself in the bathroom to wait for morning. So entranced by James, she believed his perception of herself.

On New Year's Eve, enhanced by cocaine and ecstasy, she and James went to a nightclub in a metropolitan town. Again he excused himself to the toilet, and spied on her. A man approached Laura to ask the time. James reappeared and again dragged Laura out of the club by her hair. In the taxi ride home, they fought in the back of the cab. 'Now, you be nice people,' the cab driver said. 'Stop fighting, or I get the police.'

'Back home, I tried to please him,' Laura said. They slept separately that night.

'James used drugs to control me. He kept hold of them, and I had to ask permission to use them. He gave me ephedrine and told me it would help me lose weight. I swallowed it by the handful. When I was hooked on the drug, he charged me £150 a tub.' Researching this drug I see you can buy it online for thirty pounds.

Recounting her story, my pen slid over the notepad. I glanced up at Laura and continued to write. She looked tired. I held the pen still. 'Is this reminiscing bad for your health?' I asked.

'They're things I don't want to tell you. I don't want you to know.'

'That's fine, we'll stop then.'

'No, it needs saying. I'll just have a fag.' I looked at her profile as she stood in the kitchen doorway; she blew smoke from the roll-up held close to her mouth. 'I used to think it was classy snorting cocaine up a rolled-up £20 note,' she said.

'Why always a twenty?'

'Sometimes it was a fifty, but not often.' Laura came back into the kitchen and sat opposite me. I was no longer offended by the smell of the tobacco smoke that clung to her. 'James would draw me in, then push me away.' I set the pen in motion. 'I was not allowed to go to the toilet at night, in case I woke him. If I was on an early shift, I had to sleep in the spare room, and quietly get ready for work. He was very regimented. We had to be in bed by ten-thirty and up in the morning by seven.'

'It's all about control,' I said.

'One day, I put the washing machine on before I left the house for work. When I came home, he was raging. Because the washer had disturbed his sleep.' James had smouldered on this disturbance all day.

Laura went on to tell me of future drug use. I will include that in chronological order:

Cocaine, aka coke: take me to your powerful high, please don't leave me down. You're such a potent stimulant. Why don't you ride with me for long? Temporarily speeding the way my mind and body work, you make me feel on top of the world, confident, alert and awake. Sometimes you erase me, making me over-confident, arrogant and aggressive. Changed by you, I take careless risks. When you raise my body's temperature, my heart beats faster for you. Thank you for reducing my appetite. When your power depletes, you force me on a long descent, leaving me depressed and unwell. Sometimes you force this crash to happen for days. If I have been greedy and snorted masses of your white powder and you withdraw supply, you convince me that I have flu. After snorting, why does it take a while to feel you? Yet you only stay for half an hour. Then you persuade me to inhale some more. You grab my hand and drag me to anxiety and paranoia. You evoke previous mental health issues to ride with me. Using alcohol with you increases the risk of side effects; mixed together in the body, you produce that toxic chemical: cocaethylene. You tell me to speak to White Heroin, an imposter, who makes it easier for us users to overdose. You, my friend Cocaine, have eroded the cartilage in my nose; two nostrils have become one.

Your relation Crack delivers by a different method. I smoke him through a crack pipe. His effect is almost immediate, but he only stays for ten minutes. He has gone and I am left with an intense craving for him. As he does not remain potent for long, I won't waste him in a tunnel, that's why my crack-pipe is very short. You see my cracked and blistered lips? He prefers I name them 'crack lip'. I thank him for stealing my appetite. My increased heart rate, blood pressure and body temperature are his. My contracted blood vessels and dilated pupils belong to him. We join hands in bizarre erratic behaviour; sometimes we share violence.

Hi there, I am Freebase, a method for being inhaled. Hold a flame under a metal spoon filled with cocaine (or any crushed pill). Collect my fumes from the heated crushed pills in an empty bottle and inhale me. I slither into your brain. I love this, to enter your body and destroy your soul.

Cocaine is a class A drug: illegal to have, give or sell. Possession can result in a prison sentence of up to seven years. Supplying can get you life imprisonment and an unlimited fine. A conviction from a drug-related offence can stop you visiting certain countries, the United States, amongst others. A conviction can limit the type of job you can apply for. Allowing people to supply cocaine in your house or premises can lead to prosecution. Driving under the influence of drugs can lead to a heavy fine and suspension.

Cocaine may still be in the body the day after use. Cocaine is a white powder. It has a bitter, chemical taste and smell.

Ecstasy: chemical name, MDMA: I seek out clubbers, I look for revellers. My effect takes half an hour to kick in. I work for three to six hours to give you an energy buzz. I make you feel alert, alive, super confident, in tune with your surroundings. I awaken in you amplified sounds and colours and gift you with temporary feelings of love and affection for the people you are with. Be careful, for I encourage a feeling of love and affection for strangers too. My work is all consuming. When you exhale my last spirit, I leave you with anxiety, panic attacks, confusion and paranoia. Sometimes I even choose psychosis. I can hold my power and pretend not to work, impatiently you take another 'E' and I give you extra strength. You don't really know who I am. The problem with me? Ecstasy is rarely pure, sometimes I have no MDMA at all. If you take only me, I will not turn you into a violent person. I relish mischief. I will jump in your mouth and create chatter, you will not make sense to a non-drug user. I warn you: regulate my employment, because long-term use can cause memory loss, and I can create depression and anxiety. I cause the body to release a hormone which stops it producing urine. Your body temperature rises, you are in a state of pyrexia. I readjust your body's salt and electrolyte balance. I need not tell you this, but I will, drinking water and cooling down can help you recover. I will encourage you to do this, but drink too much and danger is on the way, excessive consumption of water can cause your organs to drown. Ecstasy is a class-A drug.

Hi, I'm ephedrine, I am a prescription drug, I'm legal. I'm used to treat shortness of breath, chest tightness and wheezing due to bronchial asthma. I like to be used for other conditions determined by your doctor. I work as a decongestant, by reducing swelling and constricting blood vessels in the nasal passage. Some silly people like to abuse me because I can cause rapid weight loss. I burn fat and increase your metabolic rate.

2. REHABILITATION

The first three months of Laura's twelve-month stay in rehab were to be spent on campus. The remaining nine months she would be allowed to come home at weekends.

Map in hand, Rob and I set off to visit our daughter in rehab. I switched the car radio off when Amy Winehouse sang: They tried to make me go to rehab, but I said, no, no, no. We arrived on another tree-lined street to visit another Victorian house. Laura watched out of the window for our approach and ran to greet us. We got out of the car and stood on a coating of crisp frost. We hugged there and then, all three of us. I unloaded the goodies I had bought for her from the car.

Rob and I were impressed with the garden, a healthy outdoor space. We followed Laura into the house. A book was left open on a hall table with a pen, for an inmate to sign in and sign out. Laura led us to the dayroom where old sofas lined the walls. I could smell cooked food and taste stale tobacco, I could see ashtrays overflowing. This was in the days before the ban on smoking in shared places. I averted my gaze from a young man sat on the sofa. He was swollen, his skin an unnatural shade of yellow tinged with green: his liver was failing. A guy with a glass eye wandered into the room in his pyjamas looking for a DVD. A big lady stood up, wrung her hands together and sat down. She repeated the gestures, muttering to herself. Rob and I shared a look.

Laura took us to her bedroom, a room shared with the restless woman. My baby sleeping here with only a free-standing wardrobe to separate her from a deranged stranger.

122

I wanted to scoop Laura in my arms and take her home. I am her mother, I had a need to protect her. I convinced myself this environment would make her worse. But what could I do? Take her to a gloomy flat where she would drink days into night? Bring her home to abuse our hospitality and shake Rob's equilibrium?

Her behaviour had put a strain on our marital relationship. Rob could not tolerate Laura's behaviour and I was an emotional wreck. I huddled in a shell of worry, trying to hide from what she had become, my happiness had been destroyed. Rob resented this. It infuriated him. He worked many hard and long hours to give me a lovely home and a wonderful lifestyle. He was dumbfounded as to why my daughter distorted my pleasure.

I could not whisk her away from rehab. I had other family members to consider. Laura knew I was dying inside for her. Graciously she said, 'I need to do this. Stay here and get better.'

Oh, but how sick I was to leave her in the company of others, who in my eyes, were sicker than she. Laura was prescribed antidepressants to help with her transition. We said goodbye with tears in our eyes. I promised to visit the next week.

Rob and I travelled home in stunned silence. Back in my secure home, I put a meat and potato pie in the oven. I was lost, and needed consoling. I sat on the floor next to Rob's chair and cried, and cried some more. Rob hitched up on his seat and patted the space he made. He held his arm out. I nestled in beside him and wept. I played true movies in my head of Laura's drunken antics, of the sickness I felt with each one. I knew she needed to stay in rehab and experience what came her way.

My mind was choked with thoughts of Laura. Stacked in rows. When one scenario dispersed another took its place. To ease my mind, to banish my thoughts, I made friends with sudoku. I worked with numbers, not words, to clear my mind.

For the first three months of Laura's stay in rehab I visited every Saturday. Rob could not come, he worked most weekends. Entering the rehabilitation house, I would say hi to characters I did not want to know. To protect my well-being and blank out the reason why I was here, I took Laura out to town. We walked the vibrant streets and drank coffee in Starbucks. Chasing this normality upset me, it was a glimpse of happiness, and we would part shortly – she to incarceration, me to my miserable journey home, a house she was absent from.

A sample of life in the rehabilitation centre: The residents were obliged to dress for the morning group meeting after assigned chores were done. The manager arrived by eight in the morning and breathalysed each resident. Random breathalyser tests were carried out throughout the day. A zero tolerance to alcohol consumption was in force – one strike and you were out. The residents were not routinely tested for drugs, this was an alcohol rehabilitation service. At the group meeting, inmates were encouraged to discuss their feelings. It was not acceptable to say they were just 'okay'. This rule enabled staff and the occupants to know what the recoverer was going through and what sort of day they were having. When the meeting was over, the rest of the day was at the resident's discretion. A curfew was in place for nine at night, unless you had been awarded leave. There were no staff on the premises in the evening, at night or at weekends, though staff were contactable and lived a short distance away. Residents were encouraged to report one another for inappropriate behaviour or alcohol consumption. If they did not report, they put themselves at risk for mirroring behaviour.

On Tuesday and Thursday there were group meetings on education about alcohol. This rehab did not rely on the twelve-step guidance, it ran a cognitive behavioural therapy programme to navigate and change the way inmates thought and behaved. Yoga and mindfulness training were available on a weekly basis. It was encouraged to attend the local Alcohol Support group's drop-in sessions on Thursday and Friday afternoons to play board games and chat. Laura would often visit on women's day, where crafts such as knitting and other therapeutic activities were offered. Laura's favourite day in rehab was Tuesday. A charity scheme called Fair Share collected donated food from the major supermarkets and distributed these goods to the needy. Laura told me recently that on the day of delivery she would hoard food in her room, then binge on it and make herself sick. The bulimia had not gone away. At Christmas, Margaret, the deputy manager, took the residents shopping for food and a £20 present. Laura became close to Margaret, she shared her private feelings with her. Margaret and Stuart, the manager, became Laura's transient family. Laura began to enjoy rehab, she was comfortable in its surroundings. She had the company of like-minded people and she was not under pressure to achieve anything or manage her money. She got to do fun things, like attend a Jamie Oliver cooking course, take hypnotherapy and spend days in the park.

Every visit, I took Laura gifts to cheer her, to please me. She had been designated a room of her own. I was relieved she no longer had to share. The room had a huge bay window to let the sunshine in. The window overlooked the manicured gardens, kept so by paid gardeners, not the inmates with time on their hands. How far I had come that I would be pleased with a room in a place such as this for my daughter. Laura had a cupboard in the kitchen with her name on. I took light relief from this, I imagined student accommodation to lift my weary heart.

I bought a fridge magnet for Laura: Daughter – wherever you go, whatever you do – I will always love you. She put the magnet on the communal fridge door.

It was a two-hour round trip for me to visit Laura. With other commitments I squeezed into a week, including looking after two baby grandsons three days a week, I was exhausted. But I needed to visit her. I followed Laura into her room one Saturday morning.

After months of sick-leave from her post as a nurse, Laura was owed money: holiday pay she had not taken. The money was in my account for safe-keeping. 'I want my money,' Laura said.

'What for?' I placed a bag of items on her bed.

'To get things.'

'What things?'

'It's my money. It's up to me how I spend it.'

'You'll need money when you get out of here. You're not having it now.'

She unpacked the bag I had brought. She slammed items into a cupboard. Since coming into rehab, Laura had presented herself as a little girl lost. Now she was finding her way, she was confronting me, telling me to mind my own business. The Laura of alcohol was rearing her ugly head. I left her room and began the winding journey home.

Rob, home from work, was in the garden pulling weeds. 'You're early. What's up?'

I told him about Laura's demands. 'It's her money. Give it to her.' He stabbed his foot on the top of the spade to slice the soil. 'But she'd better not ask me for money.'

We would give money to support our daughter when she returned to her outside life. She knew this. She relied on our money for necessities, and chose to spend her money as she pleased. I gave back some of her money, not all. She was happy with that.

Rob and I sat in bed drinking hot tea. It seemed our daughter was coming back to life. She was adamant her drinking and drug taking were in the past. Rob and I discussed her present state of health and her future. Yes, she could be demanding and irrational, but that was normal for our daughter. We were ready to welcome her back, the daughter we had before alcohol and drugs claimed her. How could we make life better for her and give her a bright future? How could we ease the sickness in our own hearts? This is what we decided: buy a house with a mortgage and charge Laura a reasonable rent. I know she skipped one rental payment last time, but that was before she sought treatment, that was before she chose recovery.

Rob and I chose a house on an upmarket development, with lots of trees and grass verges. Lots of birds to herald the morning sun. We bought modern furniture and self-assembly wardrobes. We wanted Laura to be proud of what she had. Rob and I spent evenings after work, fitting the pieces of wardrobes together. Lots of instructions, screws and glue. I sat back on my heels and looked at the wooden jigsaw of furniture. I hoped we were not wasting our time. I prayed my daughter would be put back together with this accuracy: her screws nice and tight, her glue holding life together.

We bought a house and made it a home for Laura. We spent a lot of money to buy our daughter's happiness, and our own.

Laura was still in rehab. She spent her thirtieth birthday there.

Rob returned from the house for Laura with a tale of concern. 'Hey, one the neighbours at Laura's house has just collared me. He asked if I knew about the girl next door?'

'Knew what?' I asked. A giant pebble pressured my stomach.

'She attacked him with a baseball bat.'

'Attacked who?'

'The neighbour I was talking to. He said we should be wary of her.'

'You're joking?'

'He took her to court over the attack.'

'Bloody hell! We'll have to warn Laura to stay out of her way.' My poor, fragile, tragic daughter would party hard with the baseball swinger, whose name was Jo. In ignorance, we carried on.

Laura could now come home for weekends. I would collect her on Saturday mornings and take her back on Sunday afternoons. We went for walks, ate confectionery, watched movies. We had family time. We took Laura to her new house, and she was thrilled. We went to tackle her garden. Laura complained of being tired. 'Mum, I don't feel well. Can I go to your house and lie down?'

Poor girl, and silly mother who took her and left her alone. I returned to help Rob pull weeds and plant shrubs, my skin branded by brambles. What a pair of mugs Rob and I were.

Laura telephoned from rehab. 'Mum, can you come and meet Margaret, my care worker? I've told her lots about you, and she would like to meet you.' Off I went on the long journey midweek to meet Margaret the deputy manager. Laura was happy to have this get-together and this attention.

I hated to step into that rehabilitation house. It slapped me with the serious nature of my daughter's health. I felt alien to the inhabitants. I wondered if the support workers thought the same as me: that I was responsible for Laura's happiness and well-being. Mothering her had been my duty for so many years that I never considered retiring. We sat in a room, all three of us. 'Laura's doing very well,' Margaret said. We chatted politely. 'Is there anything you would like to add?'

'Yes, I want my daughter back. As a family we deserve that.' A tear fell onto my cheek.

Laura's response to my grief? 'I need to go and get some cereal, this is the time I eat.' She left Margaret and me alone.

'You know Laura does love you, she loves you a lot,' Margaret said. She handed me a tissue.

Why was I sat there, listening to a stranger tell me my daughter loved me? I knew that.

Then, Laura confronted me with an issue affecting her return to life in the outside world. She owed a lot of money: £20,000. Rob was adamant he would not mop up her debt, not this time. I worried about the effect the debt would have on Laura's well-being, on her state of mind. How could she afford to live a healthy life, and repay a debt she had no money for? An option was put to her by the finance man at rehab: declare bankruptcy.

If banks and finance companies are willing to lend money to the likes of my daughter with a history of debt, they ought to accept that debt may not be repaid. I accompanied Laura to the solicitor. She had a case. A court date was booked.

I travelled to rehab and went with Laura to court. We handed our bags over to security, and walked through the hooded metal detector, reminiscent of checking in at an airport. We sat in a room with others, all waiting for their case to be heard. I waggled my head, my cheek raised on one side. 'What's up?' Laura asked.

'The places I go to for you.' We sat, and waited for Laura's name to be called. A solicitor, not the one we had visited, ushered Laura to a different seating area. He asked a few questions. Told her to stay seated. He came back. As simple as that, Laura was declared bankrupt along with others that day. She was given a bankruptcy number as proof of the court's decision. A number to chase away the money chasers.

Laura and I left court. We stepped into the winter air, into the city with inviting shops dressed for Christmas. The twinkling lights suggested warmth and happiness. Laura stomped ahead of me because I would not buy what she desired. A smattering of her bad behaviour had returned, and stirred my emotions. She should have been linking her arm through mine, thankful to be free from the burden of debt.

Laura had an asset: a car. The court deemed the vehicle necessary should Laura return to work. Her driving ban had now expired. She was offered to buy the car at a reduced rate. Rob and I paid.

Laura had spent twelve months in rehab. Time to return home and integrate into the real world. She had reached for rehab when her life spiralled out of control, and now she had served her time and reformed. I was ecstatic at the prospect of having her home. I went to collect our cherished gift: a recovered Laura. Rachael and the boys came too.

Rob and I had discussed with Laura her need to return to work. Her year out from her career was coming to an end. Rob and I believed hard work equated to a good life. We considered it paramount for her continued recovery that she invest in her career.

I walked into the living room of the rehabilitation house, my welcome party in tow. Laura jumped off the settee to greet us. Hugs, kisses and presents were given to Laura from the care workers, the residents and the finance man. The finance man had a warning for Laura: 'Don't go back to work too soon. Make sure you are ready, that you can handle the pressure.'

What tosh! The sooner Laura got back to work the better – the whole family agreed. But we were not experts on recovering alcoholics. We had a lot to learn. Out of the building we bounced. 'Thank you, rehab, and goodbye.'

How misguided was I?

Vodka straight from the bottle

Joyous times: our daughter back home with Rob and me. Our complex, sensible, funny, happy daughter back home for good. 'Stay with me and Dad for as long as you like. There's no rush to move into your own place.' I followed her around. I hugged and kissed her. I was so happy to have her home, ecstatic to have her fixed. A couple of joyful days flew by.

'I'm just going down the street,' she said.

'Hang on, I'll walk with you. I have an errand in town.'

'For God's sake, why do I have to be with you all the time?' She slammed the door, leaving the house without me. This attitude of Laura's caused a chill to run down my spine.

In the coming days, Laura showed signs of restlessness and irritability. She decided to move into her own house and get on with her life. It was clear I needed her more than she needed me.

I bought new clothes to update Laura's wardrobe. I encouraged her to come home for meals. I visited her each day. I included her in everything I did. Her aloneness was a cause of anguish for me.

I had coffee with Laura at her house. She watched out of the window for the postman, waited for her new driving licence to appear. Her car sat at the side of her house, waiting. 'Is this postman coming today or not? This is ridiculous.'

'Be patient.' I did not like to see this agitated performance, it smacked of her previous behaviour. 'How's it going with the girl next door? The one we warned you about. You know, the one with the baseball bat?'

'Oh, Jo? She's all right. I know her from school.'

'She doesn't sound all right to me. Be careful.'

Laura continued her watch out of the window. 'Everyone has a past,' she said. True. I would not like my daughter condemned for her past. We did not know the circumstance of the attack. Was this girl provoked? Had she defended herself? We were not prepared to ask. 'Her boyfriend lives with her. He seems okay. They were drinking beers last night and asked me to join them. Don't worry, I told them about my history.'

I was pleased to hear this. I did not know it was fiction.

'The man who lives over there,' Laura pointed to a house. The same man who had warned us about the baseball incident. 'He posted me a card with a necklace in it.'

'I don't like the sound of that. Post it back.' Where in the hell had Rob and I chosen for our daughter to live? Those bricks in my stomach multiplied.

Laura chastised the phantom postman for not coming. I was an unwelcome visitor talking to the back of my daughter's head. I joined her at the window and looked out at open space, the pristine verges. But the occupants of the neighbourhood gave me concern.

A carnival was coming to town. Our toddler grandson and his mummy were in the parade, dressed as lambs. Laura was to come with me to walk along the festive float and take photographs. To watch our precious little boy. It was the day after she had watched for the postman. Laura telephoned early on the carnival morning. 'I don't feel well. I'm not coming.'

'Why? What's wrong?'

'I'm tired, for God's sake. What is this?' And there we had it. That boulder in my stomach shifted its weight. There was silence between us. I broke it.

'I've got an uneasy feeling that you've been drinking.'

'Am I always going to get this when I don't feel well? Visit and see for yourself.'

I had a couple of errands to run in town. My mobile phone rang: 'Thought you were coming to see me?'

'I am. I'll be ten minutes.' I pulled my car to a stop outside Laura's house. She watched out of the window. She opened the door before I knocked. Washed bedding hung over the living room door. 'You don't look good,' I said.

133

'I haven't been drinking. I swear.'

'Get dressed and come with me. The fresh air will do you good, and you were so looking forward to it.' Laura loves her nephews.

'No, I'm going to chill.' I interrogated her blue eyes: jet black with lies. 'I'm allowed to relax,' she said.

The carnival was a treat. The grandson was cute. I did not follow the procession to the park. I came home. I could not clear the uneasy thoughts posted in my head. Was Laura drinking? Did I have a problem? Was she drinking alcohol so soon out of recovery? Was I overreacting?

Rob and I nipped out that afternoon. I expressed my fears to him. 'If she's drinking, she's drinking. There's not a lot you can do.' Rob swung the car up our drive. Laura sat at the front door, awaiting our return. She no longer owned a key. She stood on our approach.

'Are you feeling better?' I asked.

'Yes, I don't know what was wrong with me this morning. How was the carnival? Did you take pictures?'

'Do you want coffee?' I asked, filling the kettle. I passed my camera to her.

'No, I'll get going.' She put the camera down without viewing, and off she went.

I looked to Rob. 'What was that about?'

'What?'

'Waiting for us, and then going when we arrive.'

Laura's face had looked tired, heavy makeup covered her eyes. 'She came to see how the land lies,' he shrugged.

A year later, Rachael learnt that Laura had invited serious drinkers, all of them men, for a party at her house the night before the carnival. She drank vodka straight from the bottle. 'Look at me. I've only been out of rehab for two weeks,' she bragged.

Suicide blonde

Time for Laura to refresh her career. She had a mentor to ease her back into work. Laura was back on the ward, carrying out duties. She was proud, so were Rob and I.

Laura drove to and from work. She drove up and down the High Street. She got herself about.

Saturday afternoon, Rob dropped in from work to watch the football team he supported on television. The phone's loud shrill overpowered the commentator. I answered. Laura spoke. 'Mum, can I call round?'

Ten minutes strolled by, Laura got out of her car clutching a bottle of Coca-Cola, the lid unscrewed. She placed her lips around the bottle's neck and gulped. There was an expression on her face that I was familiar with and did not like. She stepped into the hall. 'I've been drinking.' She was five months out of rehab.

I moved away from her. I sat on the bottom step of the stairs. I studied my shaking legs. Please no.

'I'm sorry.'

'I feel physically sick,' I said. I held out my hand, for her to witness the tremor.

'I know. I feel sick too.' She squeezed past me to sit on a higher stair. She allowed her secret to escape and take me prisoner. 'It's terrible, isn't it?' she said, without a hint of remorse. Like we both had done wrong, and we were commiserating. I turned to look at her.

'Go and tell Dad,' I said.

She walked into the middle of the match. 'Dad, I've been drinking.' His eyes stayed on the football field.

'Just go,' he said, 'I'm not interested.'

'Really? Do you want me to go?' Rob ignored her. She came back into the hall and looked at me for confirmation. I had nothing to say. I was incapable. She left my house, got in her car and drove away. My nerves were a jangle. I was rooted to the bottom stair. Rob rejoiced at the final score. He switched the television off. He laced up his work boots and headed for the door.

'I'll come with you,' I said.

I sat by his side in the van. I waited while he carried out his work. I did not want to be alone at home. I did not want to deal with Laura if she came back, or if she telephoned. Later, Rob jumped in the driver's seat of the van, a completed invoice in his hand. 'I feel sick to the stomach,' I said.

'I know, it's disappointing,' Rob replied.

'Disappointing! It's a bit more than that – it's heartbreaking,' I snapped. Rob thrust the gear stick into first and pulled the van from the kerb with a roar. We did not speak to each other until the next day.

Laura told me recently of this drinking binge: 'I got drunk at home on my own. I texted James and he came round after his night out. He brought a bottle of vodka and we drank it straight. He stayed the night. I drove him home late morning. He took the remainder of the vodka with him, and that pissed me off.'

136

Rob and I took a country walk. The path led to the road near Laura's house. I could see Laura heading towards us. I recognised her walk, her frame, her uniform. I did not recognise her bleached blonde hair. As our joint effort in walking brought us close, Rob and I crossed the road to greet her. 'Thought I'd have a change,' she said. Her hand lifted to her scalp and rummaged through her hair. 'I've got blisters on my head. The bleach had to stay on so long.'

Rob stared past her. He had seen and heard enough. 'Do you like it?' She looked intently at me.

'No, I do not.' Unlike my daughter, I am not very good at untruths. She pulled her hand away from her scalp. She hitched her bag up her shoulder. Laura's gorgeous, jet black hair had gone. She now had the same colour of hair as Sheena, James' live-in girlfriend. An emotion hit me like the slap of a hand, and sadness came to sit with me again. Why does my beautiful daughter, born to good looks, unique looks, want to look like somebody else? I fought hard to bank the swell of tears waiting behind my eyes. I failed. They fell down my cheeks. I looked away from her. My pain was consuming.

'What's up Mum?'

'What's the matter?' Rob asked, bemused.

I wanted to say, 'Look at her. Who is she?' But I could not. Instead, I said, 'I don't like it. I don't like your hair blonde.' Laura shrugged and walked on.

With a bottle of wine in her bag, she was eager to part company.

Voodoo wedding dress

Every waking hour I carried the burden of truth: my daughter was an alcoholic. Each night I dreamt of her as a child, before alcohol claimed her.

Many nights I was between sleep and wake. Dread bubbled in me, it would not let me rest. I would move the duvet off me and tiptoe down the stairs to make a mug of tea. I stared at the television with the volume turned off. I used to be a carefree person, I shared happiness in my life. My daughter had morphed me into a weary chassis of my former self.

I could not understand why this had happened. I must be doomed. Was bad luck in my house? Did a cloud hover over my home? I was tired. I was irrational. I honed in on Laura's redundant wedding dress, neatly folded in a box. The pure silk dress I had made with love and attention. The dress which had a cutting from her baby blanket sewn into its seam. This was the jinx which haunted us: the wedding dress. I snatched the pressed dress out of the box and tore off the tissue paper. I screwed the ceremony dress into a ball, and shoved it into the dustbin. I longed for refuse collection day. I sat back and waited for good fortune to return and bring my daughter back to me. How stupid was that?

I was painting the kitchen door. My mobile phone pinged a message. I responded quickly. The text was from Laura: sick of life, the pills and death. I read again in case panic had misguided me. I searched the house for Rob. My legs could not match the speed of my mind. He was in the garage. 'What do you make of this?' I read the text.

'Phone for an ambulance,' he said. 'Come on, we'll go over there.'

I managed to control my index finger, and punch in three numbers. 'Ambulance, please.' Rob and I arrived at Laura's house before the medics. We banged on her door. I slid the key in the lock. She opened the door a few inches.

'What?' She slurred.

'I've phoned for an ambulance.'

'I'm not going. Go away.' She closed the door in our face. Rob and I went to the car on our heightened emotion and waited. I heard the shriek of a siren before I saw the flashing blue light. Rob and I jumped out of the car as if we were laced together. We followed the fluorescent jackets to Laura's front door. She opened the door to the paramedics, and demanded her dad and I went away. We watched the scene unfold from the sanctuary of our car.

The ambulance crew coaxed Laura outside. They led her swaying body into their portable hospital and drove away. We followed the bright vehicle, forced to look at the back of the ambulance which held our desperate daughter.

Laura was shielded from the waiting room of the hospital and taken to a bed. Rob and I were ushered down a corridor by a nurse who took us to the cubicle that held Laura; the curtain was drawn. 'You'll have to wait here until the doctor has finished with your daughter.' I leant against a window of an office, I looked in at the administration paraphernalia. I tried to focus on something other than the situation. I was crumbling inside. Rob took hold of my hand and gave it a tight squeeze.

I could see Laura in uniform working on this ward, not lying in a cubicle in dirty pyjamas. The curtain hiding our daughter swished aside. The doctor exited, without looking our way or offering support. He did not share his knowledge. Was that because our daughter was an alcoholic? Did we not deserve respect? Were we part of the problem? Part of the blame?

We slid through the gap in the curtain. Laura lay on her side on top of the sheets, asleep. I placed my hand on her forehead, brushed her hair aside and kissed her. She opened her eyes. Her skin was greasy, an unfamiliar taste to my lips. A nurse joined us. Laura closed her eyes. 'We'll keep her in overnight,' the nurse said. She jotted notes on a clipboard and pulled the curtain wide.

Rob looked at me with sadness in his eyes. 'Are you all right?' he asked. I nodded. I did not trust myself to speak. 'We'll go home and leave her to come round,' he said. I took hold of Laura's tattooed foot and squeezed love into it.

Rob and I went to Laura's house to make sure it was fit for her return. There were empty alcohol bottles in every room and in the cupboard under the sink. There was a pan of stagnant pasta on the cooker, an opened packet of butter on the worktop. Magazines were strewn over the living room floor, some torn to pieces. 'It's more than an alcohol problem,' Rob said. I remained dumb. 'She's got mental health issues.' In the same way I had dismissed his diagnosis of drug use, I dismissed this assumption. What I understood: If my daughter did not drink alcohol she was sane. It was that simple in my mind. I was a fool.

I telephoned the hospital when the sun rose. Laura was fine, she would be discharged that day. I waited for a communication to go and collect her. A knock was heard on the front door. A car drove away. I opened the door to Laura. 'Can you take me to the supermarket? I need a few bits,' she said.

There was no explanation, no apology for her behaviour. There was no mention of our hospital visit. 'Can you take me shopping, or not? I can get my friends to take me if you don't want to.'

'What friends?' Laura was over the threshold. I closed the door.

'They're a middle-aged couple I met at the support group. They're coming back for me when I have done my shopping and seen you. I'm going to stay with them for a couple of days.' My daughter was a stranger to me. I did not know what she was doing, or who she spent time with.

I did as I was bid: I took her shopping. I bought a bouquet of flowers for the couple allowed into my daughter's life, the couple who usurped my role as a parent. The couple who arrived at my house to whisk my daughter away from me. The couple who tooted their horn to alert Laura. They did not introduce themselves or say hi. Laura had gone. No discussion, no hugs or kisses. No promises given that she would break.

Later that evening, Rob and I were driving home through rush hour traffic. I mulled over this latest incident in Laura's life. 'Why is she so unhappy?' I asked.

'I've no idea. She should sort herself out and get on with her career. I'll tell you what she needs, she needs to grow up.'

'I think it's James. She gets into this state when he's involved. Maybe you should go and see him. I want him out of her life.'

We arrived home. Our son-in-law, Barry, entered the house. Rob told him he was about to call on James. 'No, you're not,' Barry said. 'I'll go.' Off he went to the uninviting accounts practice. He pressed the button of the intercom. Looked up at the camera directed at his head. A message came through the intercom: Come back at six. Barry returned at six o'clock. A muscle man opened the door. James stood behind this man. Barry gave a short laugh and told James to behave, to stay away from Laura. He directed his stare at James and ignored the bodyguard.

'Laura contacts me,' James said.

'If she telephones again, ring me. I'll sort it. How would you like one of your sisters to be treated like this?'

The next day, I telephoned Laura and told her what her brother-in-law had done to protect her. She did not like that we had intervened.

The couple who had welcomed Laura as their charge had a menagerie. One member was a monkey. Laura telephoned me the second day of her stay. I heard the animals' commotion, demanding attention, just like my daughter. 'I'm going home tomorrow to clean my house. It's in a state from, you know …'

'No, I don't know.'

'My drinking binge. There are bottles everywhere.' And there it was: her admission.

'No, Dad and I have tidied the place.' She did not thank me. 'You need to sort yourself out. Put an end to this binge drinking. You're dicing with your life; you're dicing with your career.'

Laura introduced animal tales from the menagerie. She did not want a lecture; she did not want advice. She had no use for either.

Laura returned to her house, she returned to work. She visited normality, for a while. Would this experience shake her, make her realise what she was doing? Would it be classed as 'rock bottom'?

Worried, I invited Laura to stay on a Saturday night to share a meal, watch a film and sleep in her available bed. She arrived straight from work, her uniform still on. As she sat opposite me in the conservatory, we chatted. She held her wrist and stretched her arms. She perfected a yawn. 'I think I'll go home. I'm tired.'

'No, you can stay here as arranged.' I made coffee and handed her a steaming mug. She took a couple of sips then put the mug down. She looked out of the window, she checked her nails.

'I'm thinking of having my lips pumped up,' she said. She pouted to impersonate artificial lips. She knew my opinion on such matters.

'Don't be ridiculous.'

'Don't you think it will suit me?' Again she puckered up.

'Shut up.' I knew what she was doing. She would annoy me, and I would be happy for her to leave. She would provoke an argument, pick up her bag and go. I would not be goaded. She stood.

'I'm going home.' And off she went. The meal I had prepared, the sweets of her choice bought? Wasted. I could not keep her by my side if she did not want to stay. I could not protect or save her. I knew more drama was on the way.

I did not hear from Laura for days. She would not answer her phone. I did not want to visit her, to witness what I might find. Rob and I watched television. A knock on the door, unusual for that time of night. I looked through the hall window on my way to the door. I saw Laura's car parked on the drive. I opened the door. I could see she had been drinking. I could smell the alcohol seeping from her pores. I pretended not to have noticed any of these signs. 'Where are your keys?' I asked. She opened her clutched fist. I picked the keys of her palm, and took the car key off the ring. I handed back her house key. 'Go home.'

143

'Help me, Mum.' She sat on the stone floor. Her constitution could hold her no longer. My legs embraced their wobble. There was no space for the sick feeling in my stomach; stones were in residence. My poor darling girl, my baby sat on the ground, desperate for help. What help could I give? Sober her up? Offer a warm bed for the night? When the next day would bring denial and the return of her wanton behaviour. I knew I was incapable of helping her. I was useless as a mother.

Rob charged up the hall. He stepped outside and aligned his face to his daughter's face. 'Fuck off.' His voice low but clear. His fury was stronger than him. I grabbed his arm and begged him not to degrade his daughter further. With the strength of a mother, I pulled him into the house.

'Don't,' I cried.

'Then get her off my property.' I pulled him to the sitting room, guided him to his chair. His eyes were aflame. He stared at the television. I went outside to Laura and crouched by her side.

'You need to go,' I said softly. 'Please go.'

'Give me my car key,' she slurred.

'Don't be stupid. You're not driving in this state.' Though she had driven here.

'Help me, Mum, please?' If someone had pierced my heart with a dagger, it would have been less painful than this.

'I don't know how to help you. Nothing I do works.'

Laura put her hand on the outer window ledge and heaved herself into a standing position. 'Let me in. Let me in the house. I want to come home.'

How could I let her in? Rob was furious, and rightly so. Laura would goad him, try to make him behave badly, so he would be in the wrong, not her. 'No, you can't come in.' I backed away from my daughter. I kept my eyes on her. I stepped into the hall and closed the door. With a clenched fist she banged on the door, banged on the window. She banged on my heart.

'Let me in,' she shouted. Rob sprang out of his chair. I blocked his path.

'Please don't,' I begged.

'Then get her off my property. Phone the police.' I had no choice. I was in-between a raging bull and a matador. I picked up the phone and punched in three numbers.

'Please treat my request as urgent.' The receiver of the call could hear Laura shouting. He could hear Laura banging. I hid in the kitchen away from the hall window. I tried to ignore the desperation in my daughter's voice. I pleaded for the police to arrive. I huddled in a corner and closed my eyes. I did not have the ability to close my ears or my mind.

Two male officers arrived. One officer stood with Laura to question her view of events. The second officer stepped inside. Rob fixed his anger on the television, his jaw tight, his eyes black with rage. He ignored the police presence, ignored the officer stepping into his house. I closed the door to guard the entrance from Laura. 'I can see your daughter is distressed,' the officer said. 'Can you tell me what's happened?' He ignored a radio message crackling on his chest.

'We have lots of problems with her.' My voice croaked. 'She has turned up on the doorstep, demanding we rescue her. She's an alcoholic.'

'I see. It must be difficult for you and your husband.' The officer looked to the side of Rob's face, and accepted Rob's ignorance. 'Is that her car on the drive?'

'Yes.'

'Did she drive here?'

I raised my shoulders. I did not want to add to my daughter's plight. 'I have taken the car key off her.'

'Okay. What is it you want me to do? Your daughter appears to have calmed down.'

'I want you to take her away. We don't want her here. We have had so much, we can't cope anymore.'

'I do feel for you and your husband.' Again he glanced at Rob. 'It must be very upsetting. We'll take her home.'

I opened the door to let the officer out. Laura faced me. 'I can't believe you've done this to me!' She screamed.

Rob and I could not sleep the night the police took our daughter away. We were not inclined to count woolly creatures. We did what we always did: stared at the ceiling, then drank cups of tea. 'I'm proud of you, Robert.'

'What for?'

'Because Laura was trying to provoke you into a bad situation, and you listened to me and would not be drawn. If you ever treated her cruelly, I would never forgive you. She would have come between us in a way that can't be repaired. Our relationship with each other is more important than our relationship with her.' He agreed.

'We'll take her car back and post the keys through her door,' he said.

'Do you think that's wise? Shouldn't we keep the car?'

146

'I'm sick of doing what we think is best for her. Let her get on with it.'

We dressed, we skipped breakfast. Rob drove Laura's car to her house. I followed in mine. He posted the freedom keys through the same letterbox her driving licence had been delivered. Her curtains were closed, her bedroom window open. The cream curtain billowed in the breeze. Laura was home, she was sleeping, she was recovering. My heart found its natural rhythm.

Later that evening, Rob and I sat in a line of traffic. Laura was ahead in the driving seat of her car waiting in the lane which led to the supermarket. No doubt shopping for wine.

I knew I was not my daughter's keeper. I knew I was not responsible for her actions. But Laura's return to drink-driving tightened the band of tension around my head. What if she kills a child? What if she kills herself drink-driving? I am prone to these scenarios. I spoke with Rob. 'How would we feel if a drink-driver hit one of our grandsons? We both know she has driven drunk. Look, she owes us money. We could sell the car, and take the money off her debt?'

'Okay, do it.'

I had a spare key to her car. When we had lent Laura the money for a car, there had been a requirement that she hand the ownership document to me and sign it. So in the event of her not paying her loan, I could sell the car.

Early next morning, Rob and I arrived at Laura's house. I tiptoed to her car. I put the key in the ignition. The car sprang to life, a trustworthy car for a lying alcoholic.

We took the car to the garage which Rob had arranged a deal with. We pulled away from the forecourt. I had a cheque in my hand, and tension in my throat. I looked at Laura's car, waiting for its new owner. I could see my daughter in that car, in her uniform driving to work. My daughter had soaked away my well-being. She robbed me of my smile.

Back home, I made coffee. I was not looking forward to facing the wrath of Laura. I took deep breath after deep breath as my coffee went cold. It had to be done. I picked up the telephone and spoke with her. 'Right,' was all she said to the sale of her car. Was she resigned to being not trusted with the keys of a car? Or was she drunk? Who knew?

I was in the kitchen cooking an evening meal. Rob was out working. The phone rang. It was now a natural occurrence that the shrill of the telephone would tune in my anxiety. I answered. 'Is that Laura's mum?' My heart slipped on a pair of running shoes.

'Yes,' I replied to the woman's voice.

'Laura's at home, she's waiting for an ambulance. She hasn't passed urine for a couple of days.'

'Okay,' I said. I could have dropped to the floor and wept, I could have stayed there forever.

'Laura's asked that you make your way to the hospital.' I disconnected the call. I walked past the bubbling pans on the stove. I sat on the bottom step of the stairs and held my head in my hands. Was she going through the process of kidney failure? I was too frightened to move.

The telephone rang again. I wobbled over to it. 'Hi, love, I'm the paramedic taking your daughter to hospital. She wants to talk to you.' He handed the phone to Laura before I could reject the call.

'I'm not well. I'm on my way to hospital. Can you come?'

I struggled to keep the handset to my ear, my hand shook so much. 'I don't know, Laura.' I was in no fit state to drive. I knew she was in capable hands. Hardly ever did I disturb my busy husband at work. I telephoned him to update him on events.

'Attention seeking,' Rob said. He was under tremendous stress with emergency breakdowns. He did not have time for this 'shit'. I stayed home.

Rob returned late that night. He took a shower. He did not eat his meal. 'You're going to have to get your head around the fact that Laura is self-destructing and there is nothing you can do,' he said. Beads of sweat sat on his clean forehead. 'You have to prepare for the eventuality she may die. I've squared myself with this fact. I've done all I can do.'

'I can't help feeling this way.' I started to cry.

'She's making you ill. She's a selfish bitch. Get over her.'

The telephone broke the silence. Rob answered. I blew my nose. 'No, I don't have a key to her house. Don't call here again.' He hung up.

'We have a key,' I said.

'We're not getting involved. Laura has discharged herself from hospital. She's banging on her neighbour's door, asking her to contact us. I told you she was attention seeking. She would have got you to hospital, and you would have brought her back here.'

I could not stop my tears of worry.

'You do what you want. I'm going to bed.'

I followed him up the stairs.

Laura went to another neighbour, the custodian of her house key.

Family trait?

149

I spoke earlier of factors when considering alcoholism. In Laura's case, she had been left at the altar, and had issues of abandonment. She chose a career in a high-risk band regarding alcoholism. She endured a long and destructive relationship with a mind-altering man. There is a fourth factor Laura had to contend with: genetics.

Always searching for an answer, I read an article and discovered that research has shown that family history of alcoholism or drug addiction is in part genetic and not just the result of environment, peers, family, or availability. People who are at an increased risk of developing addiction share many of the neurobiological signatures of people who have already developed an addiction. People with fewer D2 receptors are more likely to become addicted than those with many receptors, and how many receptors a person's brain contains has a lot to do with genetics. D2 receptors work with the dopamine pathways in the brain, which plays a major role in reward motivated behaviour.

I considered my daughter's family history. I looked at other family members, including myself. I dissected their character traits. I regarded their alcohol intake. There was no genetic link to alcoholism. I delved further back into our lineage. I considered grandparents and great aunts, and that is where I found a genetic link.

My Nana liked a drink of beer. With an empty jug in a square wicker basket, she would leave my elder sister and me alone and nip to the corner pub. She took more care returning with the jug filled to the brim with beer, her basket covered with a tea towel. She would drink the beer during the evening. Once empty, the jug would stay that way until the next day. She was not an alcoholic, but her sister was.

My great-grandma ran away with a married man. She left the care of her children to Nana, the eldest of five. When the

150

siblings reached adulthood, Nana married. She had one child: my mum. I spent many weekends at Nana's house and saw her sisters and brother often.

The sister of Nana I refer to lost her husband in the Second World War. Great Aunt Dorothy chauffeured a high-ranking officer during the war. Clearly she was smart, capable and progressive.

When the war was over, Dorothy met a handsome Italian and they married. But he was not a good man. He offered his wife's body for hire; he became her pimp. Dorothy took to drink. I do not know if she took drugs.

When I was a child, Nana's mother came home. The romance she had traded her family for had died. She rented the house next door to Nana.

I was eight years old when Dorothy had a lung removed, due to smoking. She convalesced with her mother. 'Can I go and see Dorothy?' I remember asking.

'No, she's a bad 'un. Stay away,' Nana said.

'Mother, what a thing to say,' my mum said. 'You can go, but don't stay long because she's not well.' I skipped out of one front door and in through the next. I climbed the narrow, dark staircase of this two-up-and-two-down terraced house, with a toilet in the yard. I pushed the door to the bedroom, the sickroom. The curtains were closed. A lamp gave a halo of light. Dorothy lay on an old steel bed whose mattress afforded no comfort. The sheets and eiderdown were spotless. I sat on the stool by her bedside. Dorothy was a beautiful woman. She had jet hair and electric blue eyes in common with Laura. She told me of nights out dancing. She told me about the clothes she wore, the high-heeled shoes she loved. She described putting on her red lipstick. I listened with my head cocked to one side.

Some years after this visit, I went to the city with Mum. I saw Great Aunt Dorothy in Woolworth's department store. She wore a man's overcoat. Her flat, front zipped ankle boots had collapsed and she shuffled along. Her beautiful hair was disguised by a dirty headscarf. Mum grabbed my hand and steered me in the opposite direction. 'Turn your head forward and stop staring,' Mum said.

Six months later, on a Sunday, I visited Nana with my parents. The grown-ups were having a hushed conversation. I honed my ears. They were discussing an article in the News of the World: woman murdered, strangled and stamped on, in a flat. She was forty-seven years old. She was my great aunt, Dorothy Panetta.

Recently, I obtained my great aunt's death certificate. I wanted to know if justice had been done. She was murdered on 24 May1968. She had no occupation and the certificate notes she was formerly the wife of Anthony Panetta. The cause of death is listed as asphyxia. Strangulation by ligature. Defendant found guilty of murder but insane. I contacted the Coroner's office, and although the death certificate states an inquest date, they hold no further information on the case. Rest in peace, Dorothy Panetta.

I see parallels of behaviour. I see connected tragedy in their lives. Could Laura have a similar genetic makeup as Great Aunt Dorothy?

Then I read Tod Crandell's book There's More Than One Way to Get to Cleveland: Don't Blame Genetics – Addiction is a Choice. A choice, because many people with the same genetic makeup as an addict do not become addicts. Likewise, plenty of people without the DNA factors relating to alcoholism do become addicts. Crandell sights a study of twins carried out in 1999. The American Journal of

Psychiatry confirmed that only 50-60 percent of addiction is due to genetics.

As Crandell points out: 'Genes can place obstacles, but you can navigate around them'.

Genetics or not, I do accept there are underlying issues that make some people vulnerable to becoming alcoholic. Laura was a fast talker, a quick thinker, a rapid responder. She lived in her head, she no longer operated from her heart. I believe Laura used alcohol and drugs to blend these feelings, to bring a state of calm to her life. To forget what she had let escape. She ironed out the creases of her screwed-up brain with substance abuse. Unfortunately, alcohol did not suit her temperament. Her greed goaded her to excess. Alcoholism gripped her and she could not function without its comfort.

Todd Crandell goes on to state: 'Addiction is not a disease. The disease is the emotional pain you are trying to anaesthetise yourself against'.

Laura explained her alcoholism as a personality trait: 'It was always there. The obsessive nature of my behaviour, everything I did, I did to the extreme. I found alcohol and I liked it. I liked the calming effect. And, like everything else, I used it to excess. I do not blame anyone or anything for my alcoholism, but myself.'

Humans suffer most when they lack connection and may forge a bond with inanimate objects. Addiction becomes another person in their life and a relationship is created, which steals their focus and stops them being fully present. This relationship becomes a love affair. It is a destructive coupling, full of contradiction, and they are forced on a see-saw of life, abhorrence and enticement, avoidance and indulgence. The way to break this partnership is to confide in others.

Laura had a successful and happy life before alcohol beckoned. I believe that if Laura had stopped drinking in the early stages of seduction she could have avoided alcoholism and the destruction that followed. I am convinced that if she had not been mentally abused, her state of mind would not have decimated. And again, this is not simple. I discovered that victims of mental abuse exhibit higher than average rates of alexithymia: a difficulty in identifying and processing their own emotions, together with a problem in recognising and appreciating the emotions of others, the same traits as an addict. So was that it? Was my daughter's ability to reason compromised? Can an alcoholic recover from this mindset? Or was my daughter doomed?

Research shows that the brain would be useless if it was not changeable. Yet scientists cannot agree on what addiction is, nor how it should be categorised. Alcohol and drugs change the brain which can be both long lasting and harmful, brain scans have endorsed his. Yet some people who have suffered a brain injury discover that the neurological pathways have rewired, and bring back autonomy to the patient.

To call alcoholism a disease is to render the alcoholic as blameless, with no hope of recovery. And why the term recovery? If this is a transformation, why is the term recovered not used? It seems we are wary of the power alcohol has over the individual sufferer to ever set them free.

So if alcoholism is not a disease, what is it? A habit, a powerful habit, which is hard to break. Addiction is treated by cognitive behaviour, I am aware of this by my daughter's therapy. Where self-forgiveness is encouraged. No other disease can be cured by such a process.

It was a dichotomy: the wilful girl we had raised became selfish to the extreme. She took what she wanted, when she wanted it, leaving no room for the concern of her loved ones. Or was the girl we raised to be kind, thoughtful and moral still there? Was she sick and in need of repair?

Not interested

The telephone pierced the silence of the room. My stomach somersaulted. I dreaded what would be communicated to my ear, my mind, my heart. I took a deep breath and jabbed the acceptance button on the handset.

'Mum,' Laura's voice was quiet and low.

'What's up?' My heart won the race with my tongue.

'Work's letting me go.'

'What do you mean?' Though I knew.

'I've been asked to hand in my notice because of all the sick leave I've taken. Don't worry, Mum. I'll get another job.'

'Of course you will,' I sneered. I slammed the phone down.

Laura was preoccupied with alcohol, she had become unreliable and erratic at work. I had hoped Laura's career would be the magnet to pull her away from alcohol, but now this bait had gone. Alcohol was now her life, her career, her lover, her child. She asked if I would help her find a job online. I agreed. She would come to my house the next day to start the search.

I walked to the sitting room where my grandson played. I could not connect with him, my grandson in my care. I could not laugh at his tiger spirit.

I shared this piece of news, regarding Laura's dismissal, with Rob as I placed his evening meal before him. He pulled his lips tight, an expression of his when he held back tears.

A car I did not recognise swung up the drive. A man got out of the car, a woman stayed seated. My heart pumped faster. This was the state of agitation my daughter had put me in. I dreaded strangers calling, in the same way, I feared the telephone ringing. I worried what news they might bring to my door. I opened the door to the man. 'Are you Laura's mum?' Rob left his meal to stand at my side.

'Yes,' Rob answered for me.

'My daughter, Jo lives next door to Laura. They've been drinking together. They're in the pub now. The landlord is a friend of mine. He phoned to say my daughter and Laura are drunk.' Rob invited the man inside. 'I've just come from the pub. I took my daughter's bag from her, but then what's the point? I gave it back.'

I moved to my place of comfort and sat on the bottom stair.

'What do you want me to do about it?' Rob asked.

'My daughter's an alcoholic, her drinking has got worse since Laura moved in next door.' Though we knew this to be untrue, we did not comment. 'I shouldn't have come. I'm sorry.'

'Laura's supposed to be coming here tomorrow to look for a job online. Obviously, she won't be coming now.' I don't know why I told him. He left.

The telephone rang and a man Rob knew spoke: 'Laura's in the pub drunk, there's a bunch of men around her. I'm sorry Rob. It's just so sad to see.'

Rob rang Laura's mobile. She answered. 'What the hell do you think you're playing at? Get the fuck out of that pub and go home, before I turn up and twat somebody with a bottle!'

'You're not going,' I said. 'Leave her.' I knew there would be trouble involving the men if Rob went to defend his daughter's honour. I would not allow Rob to be at risk when Laura would carry on behaving badly.

The man who had telephoned Rob took Laura home. I spent another restless night while Laura was safely tucked up in bed.

Christmas was approaching. 'I don't want Laura to come for Christmas dinner,' I said to Rob.

'Why? What has she done now?'

'It's just … I get so upset when I see her and spend time with her.'

'That's mean, I can't see any harm in her coming home for Christmas.'

'Well, I've told her now. She's not coming. You're always telling me to get over her. This is the way I am going to do it. I'm going to distance myself.' Rob did not respond. I knew he was not happy with my decision.

A few days later I was walking with Rachael as she pushed her youngest in his pushchair. It was a miserable winter's day, and in the distance I could see Laura heading towards us in her worn fur coat. A scruffy man walked alongside her. By his side was a teenage girl. The gap between us lessened and they came close. Both parties stopped to say hello. I burst into tears. Laura looked so seedy, so unlike my beautiful daughter.

'Don't, Mum,' Laura said.

'Don't, Mum?' Rachael screamed. 'You've done this to Mum. You'd sooner be sniffing around James than worry about hurting us.' Rachael continued to shout at Laura. The man and the teenager walked away. Laura stood by my side. 'I've got to get going,' Rachael said. She was heading to playschool to collect her eldest son. 'Come with me, Mum.'

'No, it's okay.' Rachael would be busy with her boys. Busy preparing her husband's evening meal. I did not want to be an incumbrance.

'Are you sure you'll be okay?' Rachael asked. Concerned for me and anxious not to be late for her son.

'I'm fine.' I blew my nose. I shoved the tissue in my pocket.

'You're a selfish bitch,' Rachael said to Laura.

Laura walked with me on the street which would eventually lead me home. At the crossroad of our destination, Laura said. 'I'm sorry, Mum.' Her party of two were waiting in the distance. 'I am really trying. The man I'm with is a recovering addict. That's his daughter with him, she has experienced so much through his addiction. I feel sorry for her. I had such a lovely childhood.' I had nothing to say. 'Please, Mum, can I come home for Christmas?'

'I don't know, Laura. You'd better go.' The two waiting had moved up the street. Laura kissed my cheek.

'I promise I'm not drinking. Please let me come home for Christmas.'

Rob was home when I got back. He looked at me. 'What now?' My face could not hide my disquiet. I told him what had occurred, including Laura's request for Christmas. 'I can't see why she can't come for Christmas,' he said. He loved her as much as I did. He needed her home for Christmas Day.

'Fine,' I said. 'Invite her.'

Christmas Day arrived. Laura, and Rachael with her family, came home for dinner. My girls restored their friendship. The day went well.

At New Year, we were all invited to my sister's house for a party. No reason not to invite Laura. My sister's house was full of guests. There was a lot of alcohol on display. My sister has four boys, all grown men, at the party with girlfriends and mates. We played games to pass the night, waiting for twelve o'clock. Laura sat next to Rachael on a settee. I could see an uneasiness between them. I felt the strain of their lack of sisterly care. We set fireworks off at the stroke of midnight. My nephew and his mates were about to leave and go to his apartment. Laura wanted to go too. 'No,' I said. 'You're coming home with us. We've only just discussed that you stick to your arrangements.' We were trying to find our way forward in our relationship.

'I want to go with them,' she said.

'Let her go,' Rob said, resigned to the eventuality.

'Go, then. Remember you've promised to come walking with us tomorrow.' My favourite day – New Year's Day, with its gift of renewal, of starting afresh.

Lunch time the same day, Rob and I headed to my sister's house. We would go for a walk and stay for a meal. My sister and her husband were home, and no one else. After an hour passed, my nephew arrived in his car. Laura clambered out. She walked past me. 'Are you ready? Shall we set off for our walk?' I asked.

'I'm not coming.' She did not look at Rob or me. She made her way to the settee in the living room and lay down. We went for a walk without her. When we arrived back, Laura was staring at the television, a nature documentary. 'This iz Pollyanna,' she drawled, pointing a dithering finger at the television.

'What, love?' her uncle asked.

'Don't bother,' I said. 'She's drunk.'

'I am not drunk. Why'z she saying that?'

'Shut your mouth,' Rob said.

My sister appeared in the room. 'Does anyone want a drink?'

'I do,' Laura said.

'Bring her a glass of water,' I suggested. After delivering drinks, my sister went to the kitchen to prepare the meal. I followed. 'She's pissed,' I said. My sister gave a weak smile and changed the subject.

The meal was laid out buffet style. Chilli con carne, meat and potato pie, fresh cooked meats, salad and bread. The desserts were on the table with a jug of fresh cream. My sister invited everyone to dine. Laura came in last. She piled her plate high with chilli con carne, meat and salad. She picked up the jug of fresh cream and poured it over her meal.

'What are you doing?' Her cousin asked.

Laura opened her mouth, not to reply, but to shove in a fork load of food. 'You're a bloody disgrace,' Rob said. Again she did not reply, but carried on feeding her mouth. Everyone ate, trying to ignore Laura. I looked over to her. One hand was shovelling food, the other hand sat in her lap held in a fist. My baby's hand still. I could have wept, I could have screamed. Laura left the table and went upstairs. When she returned, she had her coat on, her bag over her arm. 'I've rung Dave to come and collect me. I'll wait outside.' She stepped out into the night without another word. Dave was her neighbour, the necklace giver.

'Shall we get going?' I pleaded. Travelling home in the car, I said, 'This is why I didn't want her home for Christmas. I feel sick to my stomach.' Rob did not reply.

The next day Rachael informed me. 'Laura was drinking straight vodka from a glass on New Year's Eve. She put it on the coffee table like it was a glass of water. I was fuming with her. One of my boys could have taken a drink of that.'

'I'm sorry, I didn't know. I thought it was water too.'

With my heart rate increased, I picked up the ringing telephone. 'Mum, it's me.' I waited for the next heap of rubble to land in my stomach. 'I've got a job.'

'Really? Where?'

'At a private nursing home. The pay and conditions aren't as good, but it's a job.' Breath escaped my body, my shoulders slumped. This was a problem with me: I always wanted the best for Laura. 'Don't worry, Mum. I'll prove my worth and apply for a better position.'

'No, I'm pleased,' I lied.

Rob arrived home from work. I handed him coffee. I told him about Laura's new job. He knew the nursing home, he had carried out repairs there. 'She's got a job. You have to give her credit for that,' he said.

The posting turned out to be good for Laura. She was a member of senior staff. She attended courses. But best of all, if she did not attend work, she did not get paid. She was forced into a routine. All was good, for a while.

Laura took the bus to work, she stood at bus stops in the rain. If there were no buses scheduled to match her shift, she walked home at night. I spoke with Rob. 'Shall we lend Laura money to buy a car?' I waited for his reaction, not sure what it would be. He agreed. Laura was thrilled. We scanned the local newspaper. 'Here's a good one,' I said. 'One lady owner, low mileage.'

I passed the newspaper to Laura.

'I'm not having that. It's the old model.' What was wrong with me? I should have closed the paper, I should have withdrawn the offer. Instead, I upped the budget three-fold. Rob and I took Laura to a garage. She loved the car she had chosen.

I sat in the passenger seat when she drove the car away from the forecourt. 'Do not drink and drive,' I lectured.

'I will never drink alcohol again. Can you stop banging on about drinking?'

'Fine.' She took me home, she did not come in. She was mobile once more.

Laura regretted losing her status as a nurse with the National Health Service. After six months working at the nursing home, she applied for reinstatement at a hectic ward at a different hospital. Laura confessed her history at the interview. She was asked to sit an entrance exam with the other applicants. She passed, and the job was hers. I hugged her with gratitude. She was due to start her new job in the New Year. Staff at the nursing home did not want her to leave. A night out was arranged to bid her farewell. Nearing another Christmas, the weather was blustery and snow had begun to fall. It was the night of her leaving party. 'I'm not sure I want to go,' Laura said.

'Go, you should go. You won't meet someone special if you sit alone in the house.'

'You're right. I don't want to be a dry drunk,' said Laura, using a term to describe those who no longer drink alcohol but whose behaviour displays all the patterns of an alcoholic. They act as if serving a prison sentence and cannot find joy in life away from drink. 'I'll go and have a good time, without drinking.' She dressed at my house. She wore a teal all-in-one pant suit. Her hair, once again jet, was fashionably cut, her makeup was flawless. She looked stunning. I kissed her cheek, and smelt exotic perfume. I closed the door after she left.

The same evening, our grandsons came to sleep over. Opening the curtains the next morning revealed a heavy snowfall. The virgin snow was too thick to take the boys home in the car. We wrapped up warm and set out on foot. Half an hour into this expedition, Laura pulled alongside in her car. She offered to drive us to Rachael's house. The boys were enjoying the snow, so we declined. Laura drove away, proficiently, in the wintery conditions. Why did I worry about her when she was capable of looking after herself?

When we arrived at Rachael's house, Laura opened the door. Rachael hugged her boys. We sat around the breakfast bar listening to tales from both girls' individual nights. During a chink in the conversation, Laura spoke. 'I had one Bacardi Breezer last night.' She looked to me, searched for a reaction. If Laura admitted to one drink, she would have had several.

'Not interested,' I said. I looked away from her.

Laura was excited to tell Rachael this: 'James was out last night. He said I looked beautiful.'

'You don't need him to tell you that,' I said.

163

'No, but …' she said.

'You seriously cannot be entertaining him again,' I said.

Rachael took the baton of conversation. 'Laura, you do what you want, we're not interested.' Laura's face was serene, smug even. For sure, she had spent time with her nemesis.

Before she began her career at the hospital, I went with Laura when she was fitted for a new uniform. The hospital had a sewing room with staff. Laura was kitted out with pale blue scrubs, not the traditional uniform she was used to. The colour highlighted the blue of her eyes. She looked smart, professional and capable. I was so proud.

Christmas came, and Christmas went. Before beginning her new job, Laura had to attend Human Resources for a health check because of her history. I promised to take her, to be with her for support. On the day, just before New Year, Laura knocked on my door at the correct time. She entered the hall and sat on the bottom stair. 'You don't have to come with me,' she said.

'It's okay. I said I would come.'

She rummaged in her bag. 'I haven't got my passport for identification. I'll go home for it. I may as well carry on to the hospital and go on my own.'

'Let your Mum take you, Darling,' Rob said.

'All right! I'll come back then.' She left.

'What's that all about?' I said, closing the door.

'I've no idea. I'm going to have to get going.' He kissed my cheek. Laura returned.

'I'll drive,' I said. 'You relax and prepare for your check-up.' We got in my car and set off down the road.

164

'It's not working, this,' Laura said.

'What are you talking about?'

'You and me, this relationship, it would be healthier for me without you in my life.'

'You ungrateful bitch.' I wanted to stomp on the car brakes and demand she get out. But she would miss her appointment, the restart of her career. 'Shut your mouth,' I spat. And drove on in silence.

I parked the car on a street near the hospital. We walked separately to the entrance. We passed a large house. A group of people huddled together in the garden, dragging on cigarettes. I did not read the plaque on the wall; I knew who this establishment catered for: addicts. Arms folded, we marched side by side and entered the hospital grounds. Laura turned to face me and burst into a rapid-fire of tears. 'What's the matter?' I asked.

'Nothing.' She blew her nose. Laura does not often cry in my presence. This was a shock.

'Tell me what's wrong.'

'Nothing! We'd better go in and get this over with.'

'I'm staying out here. I don't want to come with you.' I sat on a cold stone bench. I watched Laura walk toward the entrance. The automatic doors opened and swallowed her into hospital life. I took my phone out of my bag and checked the time. I looked at my watch. I re-ran the events that had just happened. I watched people enter and exit the hospital door.

Half an hour passed. The automatic doors opened and coughed Laura into the winter's air. She strode over to me with a light touch of foot 'That was better than I expected,' she said. 'They just asked a few questions. I can start on Monday.'

'So what were you crying for, and why the odd behaviour?'

'I don't know. Shall we go for coffee?'

'No, I'll take you home. It's appalling the way you have treated me.' She ignored me. She strode ahead, making her way to my car.

I suspect Laura's display of emotion was due to concern over possible blood and urine tests that would determine if she was clean. I felt a sense of unease.

Laura loved her new job. She enjoyed the thrust of busy hospital life. She welcomed the extra money. She made new friends. On the face of it, all was good, for three months.

Blossom trees

Laura began to unravel. She would take sick-leave and then appear at my house, fresh-faced and happy. Like a hamster on a wheel, repeating patterns of behaviour. She watched me strap my youngest grandson in his buggy. We took him down the street for some fresh air. 'I'm going back to work tomorrow. I feel so much better,' Laura said. 'I'm going to knuckle down and get on with my career.'

'Glad to hear it.' We arrived at green fields. I took my grandson out of his buggy, allowing him to run free. It was the month of May, a cherry blossom tree was in full bloom, a fine show of pink. Laura picked up her nephew to reach a blossom. He tugged one off the tree. I took a photograph. My grandson's lovely face was next to Laura's face. How pretty she looked. 'How many times in a lifetime do you get to see a tree blossom each spring?' I considered Laura's mortality.

'Don't be so morbid.'

Back home, I organised my grandson's lunch before taking him to play school. 'I think I'll get going.' A common phrase of Laura's.

'Are you okay?' I knew better than to ask her to stay.

'Can you lend me twenty quid?' It was always twenty, never thirty, or ten.

'No, I'm not lending you any more money, until you start paying what you owe.'

'I need money to put petrol in my car, for work.'

'Tough, I can't say it enough, start paying what you owe.'

Laura kissed her nephew. She ignored me and left the house.

Later that evening, I sat alone in the sitting room. The telephone rang. 'Laura keeps ringing and texting me,' James said.

'Okay, I'll sort it.'

'You take care,' he said with irony in his voice. I was rocking. I telephoned Laura.

'James just rang me.' Silence. 'Are you drinking?' Silence. 'Tip whatever alcohol you're drinking down the sink and go to bed. You're going to work tomorrow.' The line went dead.

When Laura had left my house she had knocked on her neighbour's door – Dave, the necklace giver – and asked for a loan. He obliged, and took her to the off-licence. Laura began a bender.

Rob and I went on holiday to relax. I tried to squeeze Laura to the back of my mind but she kept popping out in front. I did not discuss with Rob my resident feeling of worry. He would have been annoyed at the futility of my emotion. We were getting dressed for dinner. My mobile telephone rang. 'Mum, I'm sorry. I've been drinking.' I rolled my thumb over the connection button, the line went dead. It rang again. I switched the telephone off.

'Is that it now?' Rob asked. 'Is our evening ruined?'

'No,' I lied.

The next day, I switched the phone on. I ignored the voicemails left by Laura. Back home from holiday, I changed my mobile number. I did not have the courage to change my residential line. She would text the house phone. A robotic voice imparted her message. 'I have been drinking. I am sorry.' I would tremble each time that staccato voice began to speak.

I was typing at my computer when the telephone rang. 'Mum, I've been caught drink-driving again.'

'What's that got to do with me?'

'It's serious this time. I might go to prison. I need a solicitor.'

'I'm not paying for a solicitor. Sort it out yourself.' I slammed the phone down. I switched my computer off. I was sick and weary of being sick and weary. When Rob came home, I told him about Laura's message.

'Right,' he said. The following morning, we drove to Laura's house to rescue her car. Its back side window was broken. There was a dent in the side door. I turned the key in the ignition, dance music sprung to life. I took the CD out of the stereo and flung it on the passenger seat. I drove her car to my house and took her stuff out of the boot. I got a black plastic bag and shoved all her frippery into it before dumping the sack in the dustbin. Rob agreed on a price for the car from the garage we had used before. We took the car to gain a cheque and drove home in silence with sadness for a passenger. The money received for the car hardly made a dent in Laura's debt.

Laura arranged for a solicitor to take her drink-driving case. She would meet him for coffee and pay by instalment. This was 2010. Rob and I would not attend on the day of her court hearing, Laura drank half a bottle of vodka before attending court. She was asked in court if she had been drinking. She replied no. Her case was on the custodial threshold and was adjourned. Laura attended court for the second time. She was frightened at the prospect of going to prison. Friends brought her a change of clothes, suitable for a prison stay. The court decided Laura was mentally unwell and accepted her wish to return to rehab. She was given a three-year ban and a fine, no prison sentence.

Soon after the court date, I shared a coffee with Laura outside a cafe. 'I'm thinking of going back to rehab,' she said.

'I'm not going through that again. I won't be coming at weekends or bringing you home for visits.'

'Nobody is asking you to.' We sipped our cappuccinos and used a spoon to harvest the froth. We made our separate way home.

Wrapped in a shroud of worry, I was resigned to Laura's return of alcohol consumption. I saw her frequently, she appeared to be coping. Laura did not return to work. The day of the cherry blossom was the end of her career.

One Saturday, I had shopped in the afternoon with Rachael. Rob and I were due to have dinner with friends that evening. Rob was at work when I arrived home late afternoon. I opened the front door and saw a scrap of paper on the hall floor. I picked it up. I started to read. I found my way to the bottom step of the stairs. Scrawled on the paper: Very concerned, your daughter Laura is using drugs. She has a drug dealer in her house NOW. He smashed her kitchen window to gain access. I folded the note and clasped it. I raised my other hand to my mouth and clamped it there. Please come home, Robert, I repeated over and over. His van backed up the drive. I flew out of the house to be with him. 'Are you okay?' he asked. With my hand shaking, I thrust the note at him.

'Read that.'

Rob stood on the drive and scanned the note. 'I'm sick of coming home to this shit. So, we won't be going out tonight?'

'No, I'm not up to it.' Rob got back in his van and drove off. I knew where he was going: to Laura's house. I ambled back to the stairs and sat down.

Rob took a Stanley knife out of his van and knocked on Laura's door. She would not answer. He shouted, 'Open this fucking door or I'll kick it down.' Laura opened the door. She stood to the side and he went in. He charged around the rooms looking for the drug dealer. Laura was home alone. The kitchen window was smashed. Broken glass scattered prisms on the floor. Rob walked out and came home. 'She's off her face,' he said.

The next day, Rob returned to Laura's house. I insisted he not go alone, Rachael went in my place because I was incapacitated with anxiety and sorrow. He measured the kitchen window for a pane of glass, and boarded the hole. Laura sat on a chair smoking a brown cigarette, a liquorice roll up. She tried to tell Rachael about her adventure with the drug dealer. Rachael did not want to hear. Rob took Rachael home, then came back to me. 'Forget her. She's gone. She's not Laura anymore,' he said. How could I do that? I loved her dearly. I was in a miserable state.

Recently, I asked Laura to explain the smashed window, the drug dealer.

Laura: 'I was in the house next door with Jo. We were crazy drinking. When we were sober, we didn't like each other. We ignored each other. But if we were drinking, we were the best of mates. Anyway, these men from out of town came. I had met them before. It was in this company that I smoked crack. I couldn't get the hang of it at first, and it had little effect.'

My head was bent over my notepad, writing down Laura's words.

'Jo disappeared with one of the men. I was with the drug dealer in her house. Jo's dad was banging on the door. He looked in through the window, he wanted to know what we were doing in his daughter's house, and where she was. We told him to fuck off.'

I looked at Laura. Her face mirrored the shame she now felt.

'Her dad threatened to call the police, so we left. I had no key to get in my house. I asked the drug dealer to break the window. I told him, "Don't worry, it's my dad's house." Once inside, he dragged me through the shards of glass. I was covered in cuts and bruises. I can't remember the timeframe. My memory was dulled by substance abuse. I remember going to the pub with him. He had a pocket full of cash. I remember thinking, this is all right, he can buy me alcohol. I recall waking up at my house, I saw he had brought a suitcase and bags. I think he intended to stay. I started shouting at him to leave. "I'll have to ring my dad and tell him about the window. I don't want you here."'

'And what? He just left?'

'Yes, I had slept with him, I remember peeing in the bed, then Dad came.'

A month later, on a sunny Friday afternoon, my younger sister came to visit me. We sat outside and drank cool orange juice. Rachael drove her car up the drive; she had come to see her aunty. 'I've just knocked on Laura's door to see if she wanted to come. But she didn't answer.'

'She must have gone out,' I said. I hoped.

'Mm ... I'm sure I saw her at next door's window, peeping at me with a mug in her hand.'

'Jo, the baseball bat wielder,' I explained to my sister.

Rachael telephoned Laura. She took her conversation inside the house. I caught wafts of laugher, of happy chat, then Rachael reappeared.

'Did she sound okay? Do you think she has been drinking?' I asked.

'No, she's fine. She hadn't heard me knock.'

My sister said goodbye, we gave kisses all round. Rachael gave my cheek an extra kiss. She had errands to run before collecting our boys. I gathered the glasses and went inside. I did not believe the tale Laura had told her sister. I rang Laura. She was drunk, morbidly so. She had been in her neighbour's house drinking vodka from a mug. I ended the conversation. The shrill ring of the telephone shook my fragile state. 'Mum, help me, please.' I slammed the receiver down. The telephone began ringing again, each ring sharper than the last. Getting no response, Laura rang Rob on his mobile phone at work. She harassed him for the rest of the afternoon. Summer is a busy time for work. Rob was stressed with work and fraught over his daughter.

'Get on to the telephone company and find out how I block her number,' he asked of me. At that time you could not block a person using a mobile to ring another mobile. The solution was to change the mobile number. Customers were familiar with this number, so the digits had to stay. Rob identified Laura as the caller and refused to answer. But still she kept ringing. Customers could not make contact through the busy line.

For the residential line I purchased 'choose to refuse'. A code to enter after Laura rang, blocking her number from ever getting through. She would hear a message of non-connection. She rang from neighbours' phones. I blocked those numbers too.

Three days passed. My nerves were stretched to their limit. Eventually, I telephoned Laura. 'How are you doing?' I asked.

'Not bad.'

I was relieved to hear voice, relieved she was not dead. 'Mum, I'm not doing very well. Can I come home while I wait for rehab?' She was drunk. Anxiety swam with anxiety and clutched at the tension in my soul. How much more of this could I take?

'I'll ask Dad and ring you back.' Rob agreed to my request.

'You can come home. I'll telephone you at five, when the boys have gone home. Laura, you're not coming if you are drunk.'

I dashed with the boys to the supermarket and bought food that Laura would eat. I reached into a display fridge for her favourite yoghurt. My hand trembled. I dreaded her coming home. My heart was heavier than my shopping bags. Later that day, I stood by the stove stirring a sauce, my mind on Laura. Hugs and kisses and the grandsons went home. I telephoned Laura. 'I'll come now. Are you ready?'

'No, I've been drinking.'

'That's it, then, you're not coming home.' I am ashamed to say I was relieved. Every contact with Laura meant more heartache for me. I was living with anxiety on a minute-by-minute basis. I was frightened by her.

A week dragged by. I had picked up the telephone several times, but chose not to connect with Laura. Dread had cemented the stones in my stomach, a brick wall had erected to protect me, but there was still room to clamber over the top. I picked up the telephone again, I made a connection with her. She was hardly coherent. She did not want to live.

I telephoned our GP during surgery hours and told him about the situation. 'Take her to Accident and Emergency,' he said, with sorrow in his voice. 'It's your only option.'

'Laura, I'm coming to collect you to take you to hospital.'

'I'm not going to hospital.' Laura had gone through numerous supervised detoxes at home, sanctioned by our doctor. Several times, unbeknown to me, Laura had been admitted to hospital. The hospital where she used to work. Staff she had worked alongside cleaned her body of excrement. She was ashamed.

'Please,' I said. 'Let me take you to get some rest. To get away from alcohol.'

'No!' Laura terminated our contact.

I could have been sick. I telephoned the local alcohol service team and left a message on their machine. My request for help was ignored. I telephoned again. I spoke to a man. 'We can't get involved without your daughter's consent.'

Support is for the alcoholic. Who would help me? 'Please, is there anything you can offer? I am desperate. She is waiting to go into rehab, but I fear she will be dead by then.'

'Go to the Salvation Army. They will take her. But they have a strict regime and it doesn't suit everyone.'

'The Salvation Army will take you. I'll come for you and drive you to the nearest one.'

'I'm not going there. I won't be able to wear makeup, read magazines, or have a boyfriend.'

'What?'

'I'm not going there.'

'I give up. You get on with it.' Though I said this I did not feel it. I was wretched.

Two weeks slid by. I sat in the conservatory and watched the sun descend. Rob watched football on the television in the family room. His mobile rang, primed for customers, he answered. 'Can you come and sort your daughter out? She's locked herself out and is asleep in her front garden.' Rob's lips pulled the tight line they were now familiar with.

'Do you want me to come with you?' I asked. Desperate for him to say no.

'You stay here. She's a pain in the arse.' Goals were scored in his absence.

I sat on the edge of the settee. My leg tapped out a tune of fear. I was not able to put the kettle on for a cup of tea. It took forever before Rob came home. I jumped up to open the front door to him.

'Well?' I asked.

'She wasn't locked out. She's pissed. She followed me up the street, clawing at my leg and begging to be brought home.'

'Oh no!' Please God, no.

'She's in her pyjamas. Pissed,' he said, again.

'What did you do?' I could hardly bear to hear the answer.

With a choked voice, he said, 'I told her to fuck off. She was clawing at me like an animal. Clinging to my leg.'

'It's awful, isn't it? But what can we do?' Rob ignored me. He switched the television off. The house phone screeched. A different neighbour of Laura's said our daughter needed help. The telephone rang again, and again. The business line chimed. Rob's mobile telephone sprung into tune. For the first time ever, we unplugged all telephones. Not an easy decision, when our business offers a twenty-four-hour service. We switched off all the house lights, and let darkness prevail. We sat mortified in the conservatory, staring out into the dark. We were numb with fear, numb with sadness. I wanted to run away, to hide, but that was a step too far for Rob. We went to bed, and waited for morning.

We got out of bed when sunlight allowed. Deep sorrow claimed us. We pushed back tears. I swallowed a dry throat. Barry, our son-in-law, came into the house. I switched the kettle on. I told him about the previous evening. Rob fixed his eyes on the window, tears rolled down his cheeks. Tears rolled down Barry's cheeks. We were desolate, Rob and I. We went to visit the doctor; he prescribed antidepressant medication for Rob. I was taking it already.

The doctor offered the service of a counsellor, and we both declined. He picked up the telephone and spoke to a receptionist, told her to chase the admission for our daughter entering rehab. Back home, Rob went to work. I sat in the house, frightened and alone. I sat on the bottom stair, petrified of the silent telephone.

Laura improved. She realised we would not be manipulated. She waited for her slot in rehab. The hold-up was due to her insistence on returning to the same establishment as before. During this period of waiting, a male neighbour of Laura's helped her to do chores. He helped her in a way I could not, he helped without judgement.

Rob and I walked down the street. Laura's neighbour helper drove past with Laura in the passenger seat. She insisted he stop the car, she got out and ran towards us. 'Is it okay for me to come up to you like this?'

'Of course,' I said. Rob remained silent. Laura flung her arms around me. I hugged her skinny frame. There was no substance inside her being. I could have sobbed for mercy.

'I'm waiting for one person to leave rehab. I should be going in soon.' She held out her mobile phone. 'I'm just waiting for the call.'

'Ring Dad when that happens.' Laura smiled at her dad. He smiled back and kissed her cold cheek. We walked away. I could not bear to look back, to see her get in an unfamiliar car, to watch her travel farther away from me. Rob and I turned a corner in the street, we had not turned a corner of our emotions.

My daughter was dying, I was convinced of that. What could I do that I had not done before? I needed her far more than she needed me.

Laura was going to rehab for another twelve-month stay. There would be no visit to a detox centre. She asked that we collect her belongings and store them in the old familiar black sacks.

Had Laura sought a stay in rehab for her alcoholism? Or was she escaping debt and responsibility? Had she sought treatment to escape a prison sentence for her second conviction of drunk driving? Either way, her going to rehab was respite for me, for the whole family. I could relax. However sad it is to have your daughter in such an establishment, it is safer than having her out on the streets, drinking. I could breathe again. How different my outlook compared with Laura's first stint in rehabilitation. Now I was happy to have her looked after and cared for, and for her not to be alone.

Virtual life

Rob and I collected Laura's belongings, but it was not as harrowing as the first time she went to rehab. Then we let the house, fully furnished. And along they came – the tenants from hell, a young couple, with his mother by his side. The mother could not thank us enough for the lovely property we supplied. She paid the deposit. 'People never give young people a chance, thank you.'

Strange comment then, not surprising now. I'll come back to their behaviour later. In the meantime, Laura welcomed rehab. The same staff as four years ago were employed. Her transient family would save her. She could be childlike in their company.

Laura knew the procedures of rehab, and what she was entitled to. She reigned supreme. Laura loved to talk about her feelings, the luxury of having someone listen to her every word, without condemnation. Criticism was levelled at her, but in a light way, not the way I spat it out. Laura easily made friends. She made friends with a married woman, Nat, in rehab. Her husband took both women out, to the park, to the theatre, and shopping. A rapid friendship brought the two women close.

From my perspective, Laura was having the time of her life. I do not think rehabilitation should be such a positive experience. Fine that you are counselled and encouraged to interact, to cook for yourself, and to step outside without visiting an off-licence. And, of course, the abstinence of alcohol is an excellent thing. But to enjoy the experience more than life in the real world? At the time, I would have preferred Laura's stay to have been more of a deterrent. I was wrong.

Now, I realise that Laura was wounded. She needed this shelter and support to repair. She needed to feel happy and wanted. To be a part of something.

I gave my mobile number to Laura. I unlocked her number from my residential line. Life was good. With the aid of Nat, Laura discovered Facebook. She reconnected with old friends and found new ones through recommendations. Her virtual life had begun.

Rob and I collected Laura on this Christmas morning to bring her home for a few days. I was so excited to have her stay. I gave her wrapped gifts, chosen with care. She was tired and wanted to go to bed. I woke her early in the afternoon. Time to go to Rachael's for dinner.

We enjoyed Christmas Day, the enthusiasm of the two young boys. We laughed at the white terrier ripping paper off presents not meant for him. Back home, Laura went to bed. 'What do you think?' I asked Rob.

'About what?'

'Laura, does she seem all right to you?'

'She's quiet.'

'You'd have thought she would be thrilled to spend this time with us. Instead she goes to bed.'

'Who knows what's going on inside her head?' He laughed at a comedian's joke on television.

I turned my head to the programme. I did not laugh. The next day, Laura wanted to return to rehab.

We picked up Laura from rehab on New Year's Eve. We went to a party at Rachael's house. The family drank alcohol. I did not, out of respect for Laura. 'Mum, this is going to be my year,' Laura said, on the stroke of midnight.

Laura hooked up with strangers on Facebook. I answered the telephone. 'Hi, Mum, can I come home this weekend?'

'Sure, what would you like to do?'

'I've made arrangements with Kelly. There's a crowd of us going out on Saturday night.'

'Okay …'

'I'll sleep at Kelly's Saturday night. She doesn't want to stay out late. She's taking her son to football on Sunday morning. I'll only drink soft drinks.' I knew Kelly, she had been a student nurse with Laura. They had shared much laughter. Kelly was a hardworking and caring mother. A perfect chaperone for Laura.

As agreed, I brought Laura home from rehab. We wandered down the street, we went for coffee. The wave of hands and a few hi's greeted Laura. I was pleased people welcomed her.

Laura placed her clothes for the evening on her infrequent bed in my home. She took a bubble bath and got dressed. She looked beautiful in a burnt orange slinky dress. I drove her to Kelly's house. I waited while she rang the door bell. I waved to Kelly before driving away. Laura was having a taste of her life when it was good. My heart smiled.

Laura was due back at my house early next morning. Eleven o'clock stretched into twelve and still no sight of her. Even though it was Sunday, I got the ironing board out of the cupboard and sorted the laundry. I needed to occupy my mind. Rob was gardening. The telephone rang at one-thirty-five. 'I'll be back in an hour,' Laura said. My apprehension grew stronger.

Kelly brought Laura home. Kelly did not wave to me. Laura pushed past me in the doorway, went upstairs, and came down with a rolled cigarette. She sat on the patio outside to smoke it. I watched her through the window, she stared back at me. She stubbed out the cigarette, leaving a charcoal stain. She flicked the tab onto the ground. All of which she knew I would disapprove of. She found her dad in the garden. He had no inclination to smile at her puffy face. She stormed into the house. 'Dad thinks I've been drinking.'

'Have you?'

'No, I have not. I'm sick of this. I'm doing really well. Can you take me back?'

'You want to go now?' The meal I had prepared, the evening I had looked forward to?

I turned the key in the car's ignition. 'So, what did you do last night?' I asked.

'Nothing, I was in for ten.' Laura rifled through my CD collection, chose the Black Eyed Peas, pushed into the slit on the dash. She turned the volume up high, leant back in the seat and closed her eyes.

The next day, I switched my computer on. Laura had used it to log onto Facebook, but she had not logged out. I should not have scoured her page but I did. There it was, an indication of Saturday night's events. A picture of a random guy with Laura. I clicked onto his status. He had posted about his nightmare night. Wished he had not gone out to meet Laura. I telephoned Laura, told her what I had found. I stopped short of accusing her of alcohol consumption. I did not want her to be kicked out of rehab.

I visited Laura on my birthday. It was a hot summer's day. We dined at a little bistro. We meandered in and out of the shops. We walked the tree-lined street. People mingled, they had purpose. They shared what appeared to be a normal life. Why, oh why, could my daughter not be like my perception of them? I stopped and turned to face Laura. I began to cry, huge heavy sobs. 'What's up, Mum?'

'This, you,' I managed to piece together. 'I wanted so much more for you.'

'Mum, don't, I'm fine. I'll come out of rehab and go back to work. I'll be good. You'll see.' I blew my nose. I nodded in her direction. I held my lips between my teeth to contain my emotion. I did not trust myself to speak.

We sat in the garden of the rehabilitation facility. 'I think I'll make my way home,' I said. Laura jumped off her seat. She was ready for me to go. She walked with me to my waiting car. I hugged her goodbye, and could not contain my tears, they ran faster than before.

'Don't, Mum.'

'I can't help it. I feel so wretched for you. I worry so much about you.'

Sadness dulled her eyes. 'Ring me when you get home.'

I drove the car around the corner and yanked the handbrake on. I sobbed myself dry. Back home, I found a book to bury my head in. I had so much stress to deal with.

Rob returned from work. 'What's up? You look ill.'

'I've been upset today on my visit with Laura.'

'What's she done?'

'Nothing, I just, you know … her situation. The way she lives.' Tears rolled down my face.

'I thought you'd got over this.' His eyebrows lowered. He was in no mood to console me. I did what I always did: I took a spade and buried my feelings underneath the erected wall inside of me. I smiled with my mouth and steadfast eyes. 'You look like an old woman. She's not worth getting upset over.' He went upstairs to take a shower.

Some weeks later, Laura telephoned. 'Mum, I've been seeing someone.'

'Have you? Who?'

Laura had accepted a friend request on Facebook from Mike whom she knew from school days. I knew of Mike. 'Isn't he living with someone? Don't they have two children?'

'Yes, but they don't love each other. Anyway, have you spoken with my cousin?'

'No, why?'

'I bumped into him at a hotel in the city. I had gone for the weekend with Mike.' My mind raced to a bar in a hotel. Did Laura sit there drinking cocktails?

'I doubt very much your cousin would tell tales on you.' Part of me was happy Laura had a companion to spend quality time with. I could picture her in a joyful place. But how could this relationship last? He had children, and Laura was a full-time occupation. My happiness swapped with disappointment when I realised my birthday was spent distraught over her loneliness, while she was basking in new love. She could have chased my pain away that day. She chose not to.

Recently, I visited Margaret and Stuart at the rehabilitation establishment where Laura had stayed. I interviewed them jointly to get a flavour of rehab from their perspective.

Stuart is a therapeutic worker with twenty-five years' experience. He looks in his fifties. Margaret, also in her fifties, has twenty years of knowledge at the same establishment. Both are recovering alcoholics.

Me: 'Who provides funding? The government or charity? What percentage of clients pay privately?'

Stuart: 'Funding comes under the umbrella of social services. In the twenty-five years I have worked here, you can count on one hand the people who paid for care privately.'

Margaret: 'We are trying to attract the fee-payer. I think it's lovely here, look, we have new carpets and furniture.'

I look around the room, Margaret is correct.

Stuart: 'In my opinion, people paying for rehab think they don't have to follow the rules. We wouldn't accept that attitude here.'

Laura was content and happy to stay in this environment. I could not have paid for better care.

Me: 'What is the success rate of sober living after leaving rehab?'

Margaret: 'It depends how you measure success. Are they successful if they stay sober for six months? It may be that a person has lapsed, but they are supported in the system. Eighty per cent of residents have mental health issues. They use alcohol to self-medicate. We identify their health issues, get them clean, and introduce them to the mental health service. We offer support when they leave; we have a drop-in day on Tuesday for anyone who needs to visit. We provide a wrap-around service on leaving rehab. The take-up for the service is high. I consider this to be success.'

I see now there are degrees of achievement. I had assumed Laura would be fixed after her first stay in rehab. That she would not risk her life twisting out of control again. That she had learnt her lesson. I did not consider her grief or what mattered to her. Alcoholics repeat patterns of behaviour. It was not surprising Laura would find herself back in rehab. Her journey was incomplete.

Me: 'What age and gender is the most prominent for entering rehab? Has this changed over the years?'

Stuart: 'Twenty-five years ago, we had what I would call the Good Old Boys. Aged between late forties and early sixties. They didn't live much longer than that. It was extremely unusual to have a female enter rehab at that time. Back then, the residents would be unemployed with no fixed abode. We called them the double dolers: they would check into rehab for two weeks and claim dole money. Leave rehab and claim dole for a second time from another area, for that same period. They used rehab to recuperate. You have to remember that these people had lost everything. They had no motivation to improve their situation. They came to us to save money and have a rest. They did not rehabilitate.'

Stuart looked out of the window, then brought his attention back to the room.

Stuart: 'Now we are seeing people in their early twenties and from all walks of life. There is not the stigma attached to alcoholism as there was in the past. As a result, people seek treatment earlier in their alcoholic career. They take rehabilitation more seriously.'

Margaret: 'Treating women is more complex than treating men. Women carry more guilt. They have children taken away from them. After six months, these children are being put up for adoption.'

Me: 'So soon?'

Margaret: 'Yes, it happens a lot.'

Everyone suffers in the grasp of the alcoholic. I could not understand how alcoholism had claimed my beautiful daughter. I was angry with her for her wilful destruction. I used to think alcoholics were older, weary of life. Failures in their choice of career, and relationships. I was wrong.

Me: 'What is the majority ethnic race you provide for? Has this changed over the years?'

Margaret: 'White British, we have very few other races. We employed someone of mixed race, and also an Asian, to try and encourage their ethnic race to seek treatment. But it didn't work. Though one lovely man we treated was from Venezuela. He was the one who came up with the idea of the drop-in service we hold on Tuesdays.'

Stuart: 'Culturally it is difficult for people of varying religious backgrounds to seek treatment. They would be ostracised by their community, not only for alcoholism, but because they made this trait public. This would bring shame to the whole family.'

I was not ashamed of Laura. If alcoholism could grip my beautiful, much-loved daughter, it could grab anyone and take them hostage. Who knows what goes on behind any closed curtain.

Me: 'Is it helpful to have suffered addiction to do the job you do?'

Stuart: 'I always answer that question by asking, "Does a surgeon, operating on a cancer patient, had to have suffered cancer?" Being an addict does give you empathy with the condition others suffer. People who are not recovering addicts can make wrong assumptions about alcoholics. Alcoholism is just a label. No two addicts are the same. We treat them as individuals.'

Margaret: 'No, it is not necessary to have the experience of being an addict, though it is helpful to have that insight.'

Laura gained insight into alcoholism through experience. I have gained insight into addiction through her struggle.

Me: 'What is the average term people stay in rehab?'

Margaret: 'We use to offer a twelve-month stay, but due to funding being reduced, we now offer a six-month stay. The majority of people who come to us stay for the full term. But, we have a zero tolerance policy. We carry out breathalyser tests every day. If anyone fails the test, they are evicted. We have to consider other residents. If one resident is drinking alcohol, that person puts the others at risk. We also carry out drug tests if and when we think necessary. But we are an alcohol rehab, not a drugs rehab.'

Although it was an obvious deterrent for Laura to be breathalysed each day, it was the acceptance of Stuart and Margaret of her as a person, not an alcoholic, which helped her.

Me: 'As a society, what can be done to reduce the drinking culture that has now developed, and accepted as the norm? For instance, speeding on roads has reduced due to speeding fines and heavy penalties.'

Stuart: 'This is a tricky one. The government receives huge revenue from the tax on alcohol, revenue they would not want to lose.'

Laura grew up in a culture of drinking, of displaying laddish behaviour. Her friends behaved the same. Her friends were able to walk away from this stage of their life. Laura was not. If this drunken behaviour was openly frowned upon, would this have saved my daughter? Would she be able to moderate her intake of alcohol to comply with her company?

Me: 'Are you at risk from becoming too involved with recovering addicts in your care?'

Margaret: 'Sometimes. I love Laura, so I had to withdraw from her as it came time for her to leave. I miss her. But generally, you don't allow yourself to get involved. Alcoholism creates a lot of sadness. You have to protect yourself. There are a lot of funerals to attend.'

Stuart: 'You try not to invest in people straight away, because not everyone has good potential.'

The thought of Laura brought a smile to raise Margaret's cheeks.

Margaret: 'We didn't mind when Laura took all the pies to her room on Fair Share day.'

Laura's bulimia raises its head again.

Me: 'Alcoholics are selfish. Do you become frustrated with this trait?'

Margaret: 'You have to be selfish to become a successful addict. And, yes, we deal with a lot of selfish people. We are used to this behaviour.'

Alcohol turned my daughter into a self-indulgent being. Prior to drinking, she had been kind and generous.

Me: 'What is your view on alcoholism? Is it a choice or an illness?'

Margaret: 'It's learnt behaviour and a choice. People drink on emotions, it's a quick fix. Alcoholics are lost, they look to find themselves, and they do this through drinking. They search to fill a void, but they don't realise the void is in them.'

Stuart: 'I don't believe it's an illness. It's a choice driven by the need to cover other issues.'

I think of Laura and her sorrow for everything she had lost. I think of her choosing alcohol to forget. To help her care less.

Me: 'What is your opinion on genetics? Do they play a role in alcoholism?'

Margaret: 'Learnt behaviour runs through families, so yes in that respect I agree. But, no, alcoholism is not inherited.'

Stuart: 'If you have a genetic illness, you rely on someone to repair you. An alcoholic has to repair themselves, you cannot do it for them. To suggest a genetic illness is suggesting there is nothing you can do to help yourself.'

Laura could have walked away from alcohol before it became a problem. She chose not to.

Me: 'Do you consider your job a vocation?'

Margaret: 'Yes, definitely, it gives meaning and purpose to my life.'

Stuart: 'I work a lot more hours than I am paid for. Yes, it's a calling.'

My questions had come to an end. Our conversation had not. Stuart suggested that if alcohol were to be categorised today it would be a class A drug. He went on to say that eighty percent of alcohol was drunk by twenty percent of the population. Margaret advised me to look up Alcohol Concern, the national charity focusing on alcohol, for facts and figures relating to alcoholism. Stuart and Margaret look back on their careers as alcoholics and share with me a snippet of their experience.

'I was so far gone into my drinking,' said Stuart, 'that when my wife said she was leaving me, I told her she needed help. I thought she was sick. I wouldn't even allow my son to ride a bike. I couldn't cope if he hurt himself. I bitterly regret that I took my child's childhood from him.'

'Yes, that's right,' said Margaret. 'I wouldn't let my son climb trees for conkers for the same reason.'

Then Margaret looked at me and said, 'You're a different person to the one we met on Laura's first stay. You seemed uptight and insulated.'

I admitted I was suffering back then. I couldn't cope with the concept of my daughter being in rehab.

Stuart and Margaret are two people who have reclaimed their lives from alcoholism and put their experience to valuable use for others.

Laura's twelve-month stint in rehab was drawing to a close. Rob and I refused to take responsibility for her accommodation. The authorities found a place for her to live. Before she moved into this flat, Rob hired a van. We were between tenants in the house that held Laura's furniture. We loaded the van with her belongings and set off to find where she would live.

Outside the property that would be Laura's accommodation, anxiety came to surf with me again. I know decent people are unfortunate to live in such a place, but it was crawling with low life. We walked down a slope of steps, a handrail for support. We went through a door into a concrete alleyway. A broken light hung overhead. A dank smell hung in the air. Concrete stairs climbed to dark shadows. The door facing our entrance was metal and bolted shut. A plant in full bloom sat on its step. I shared a look with Rob. On our immediate right was Laura's door. We entered her flat and closed the door. In and out of rooms we walked: a bedroom, a bathroom, a kitchen and a living room. A glass door unit to the outside, with a broken lock, was draped by a dirty ripped net curtain. I pulled the curtain aside and looked through the hazy glass at the overgrown, shared garden.

We unloaded Laura's stuff. I tried to remain upbeat. Laura wiped out cupboards, ran a cloth over the worktop. 'Look at this, Mum.' I peered at an identity card. I had left my reading glasses at home.

'What is it?'

'Must belong to the man who lived here. He's a prisoner out on parole.' My distress was tripping over hurdles, each one higher than before.

Time to leave. Laura closed the door. I looked again at the metal door. I feared for my daughter's safety and for her recovery. Rob and I took Laura back to rehab. Her stay, though coming to an end, was not complete.

Back home. 'It's dreadful where Laura is going to live, isn't it?' I said. Rob sighed and fought hard to contain his emotion. He did not say, or need to say, anything. He was devastated. Who would help our daughter when we were forced to step out? 'But what can we do? Buy a place for her to live, and go through everything we went before, twice?' He nodded at my observation, his lips tight. 'It might be good for her living there. It might make her realise what she has lost. Encourage her to strive for better.' I did not believe my words. I was consumed by fear regarding my daughter's future. I knew living in such a place would cause anyone to seek relief with the help of alcohol, or drugs.

When I had sorrow for Laura, I saw her as the child she used to be, the funny, loving girl she became, the beautiful caring adult she really was. I did not see her as a hard, untrustworthy alcoholic.

Quivering with fear for my daughter, I went to visit the doctor, the doctor who knew and had tried to help Laura. I attempted to explain my feeling of desperation. I told him of Laura's living conditions. I started to cry. He handed me a tissue. 'It must be very hard,' he said. 'She is your girl.' My doctor had just welcomed a newborn daughter into his life. 'Would you consider counselling? I know you have refused in the past, but it can be beneficial.'

I would do anything to ease my state of mind, so I agreed.

Some weeks later, I attended a referral meeting with the mental health team to determine whether counselling would benefit me. Rob was against this appointment. He was convinced notions of my wrongdoing would be fed to me. He thought counselling would make me worse. I sat opposite a young woman. 'Your doctor has referred you. It says here that you don't like where your daughter lives.'

'It's a little more than that!' I told her the life I had been forced to live alongside my alcoholic daughter. The young woman jotted notes on a pad, looked up at me occasionally. After consideration, she booked me for a course of treatment. She handed me three pamphlets on stress, anxiety and depression published by the Mental Health NHS Trust.

I absorbed the information given by this literature. Advice on recognising a disorder, and steps to avoid a condition from escalating. What I identified: I was repeating patterns of bad imaginings, all of them morbid, yet none of them had happened. I needed to train my mind to think in a positive way, not swamp my head with visions of my living daughter's funeral.

I lay my head on the pillow at night and forced concentration on my grandchildren. I replayed their happy moments. Determination saved my thoughts from wandering to the dark place Laura beckoned. It helped.

I was allocated ten sessions of therapy with a counsellor. I set off for my first appointment. I filled out a questionnaire on a computer. I explained my situation. I cried and cried some more. The counsellor listened. Back home, I took painkillers for the migraine that had developed and went to bed. The following week, remembering how unwell I had felt, I popped a couple of painkillers before my appointment. I was encouraged to discuss why I was so bereft. I told the counsellor what Rob and I had provided, what we had done for our daughter. What we refused to provide now. How desolate that made me feel. 'How old is your daughter?' she asked.

'Thirty-four.'

'You are not responsible for her. She is an adult. You have done an awful lot for her, and yet she continues to be destructive. You are not accountable for her behaviour.'

To be told this by a person in authority! A chance to breathe a lighter breath. This was a huge boulder lifted from my stomach. I was Laura's mother. I shouldered the responsibility of supporting her, and it was too heavy a burden. Yet the counsellor allowed me to abandon this weight. I walked out of that session taller than I had walked in a long time.

I attended four sessions out of ten. On leaving the room on the last visit, the counsellor said she admired me for all that I had done, for how I had coped.

I shared my sessions, relayed them to Rob in the hope of helping him heal. That evening, I told him of the praise afforded me.

'She'll say that to all of them.'

'Thanks.' But I knew he was pleased. His wife had not had her head stuffed with doubt and obligation.

Rob and I went to visit Laura in the flat we hated. We took her a winter coat. A style she would have chosen. Her face did not hide the abuse of alcohol, though she tried to. 'I'm tired. I don't feel well. I'm going outside for a cigarette.' She would not smoke in our presence.

'We'll get going, if you're not well,' I said.

'Okay.' We had only just arrived. She did not want us to stay. She asked for money. We refused. On the journey home, I had nothing to say to Rob.

To ease my concern for Laura, I ordered groceries to be delivered to her once a month, food I knew she would like, and toiletries, with treats thrown in. I was informed by a social worker this was not a good thing to do. 'For one, it frees her own money to buy alcohol. And for two, where she is living, the grocery truck will bring other residents flocking.

Like flies to shit.' It seemed everything I did was the wrong thing to do.

My daughter, once again, was slipping down the slimy slide to ruin. I telephoned her often. I visited occasionally. The affair with Mike was over. Laura was heartbroken. Apparently, they really loved each other. Another time, another place, they would have been together. Today she tells me, 'In the end, he took the role of a care worker. It wasn't a healthy relationship, and I resented him for not rescuing me. I was drinking to excess.'

Rob and I returned from holiday. I rang Rachael and listened. 'I didn't want to tell you, but Laura has been self-harming,' she said.

With the telephone pressed to my ear, I found my way to the bottom stair and sat down. 'What do you mean?' Alcohol, drugs, bulimia are all self-harming choices.

Rachael had sat in a taxi on Friday evening with her husband and two boys. They were off to a celebration. Rachael answered her mobile phone to Laura, who screamed down the phone: 'I've slit my wrists.' Rachael disconnected the call and turned her mobile off.

My conversation with Rachael came to an end. Rob knew by my demeanour that there was a situation. I explained. Rob telephoned Laura. She was morose over Mike. Rob went to visit her. I did not have the constitution to go with him; my fear and anxiety locked me inside the house. I was forced, for my own well-being, to detach from her. He asked Laura to show him the scars from her slit wrists. She could not, there were none. Attention seeking? Or was it desperation? Which is harder to accept?

Sometime later I was cooking the evening meal and Laura phoned. 'Mum, I've been burgled. Everything has gone. Even the laptop. I hate it here!'

'Have you phoned the police?'

'Yes, I've got a crime number.'

'How did they get in?' The image of the glass door with a broken lock zoomed into my head. The tale she fed me did not stack up. I switched the knobs on the cooker off. I sat down. I stood up. I looked out of the window. I sat on the bottom stair and waited for Rob to come home. 'Laura's been robbed.' He still had his work boots on.

'Bollocks, she's sold her stuff for drugs.'

'I don't think so. She uses her laptop for Facebook.' I was always in denial. I wanted to calm myself. Which is preferable: your daughter lives miles away and she had been robbed, or she sold her belongings for drugs?

'If she's not sold them, they've been taken off her for a drug debt, probably by him with the metal door,' Rob said.

I reinstated the uncooked meal. We ate in silence. The screaming of the phone butted in. 'Mum, someone has scratched grass, with a skull and cross bone, over my door.' I pacified her, as best I could.

'See,' I said to Rob, when I had put the receiver down. 'She's not safe. I hate her living there.'

'What do you want to do?'

'I want to find somewhere else for her to live, somewhere decent, a private property. We can pay the deposit and first month's rent.' He agreed. He did so for his daughter and me.

Years later, I learnt that the man with the metal door had asked his girlfriend to knock on Laura's door. She was invited inside. 'I was frightened by her,' Laura confessed. 'She was a hard girl.' The girlfriend cracked open the glass door when Laura went to the toilet, preparing the way for an easy break-in. When Laura went out, the Metal Door Man and the Hard Girl broke in and robbed Laura of her belongings. What a shit hole to be living in! Why do the authorities place vulnerable people in such precarious environments? The government spends thousands on rehabilitation, then cuts the rehabilitated adrift to struggle in the worst possible conditions.

Recently, I asked Laura to tell me her experience of living in this awful place. At the time of her being there I did not have the constitution to seek this knowledge.

'Margaret drove me from rehab to the flat,' Laura began. 'She wished me well. As soon as she had gone I went out and bought a bottle of vodka.'

This I can understand. It was a hell of a place for her to live.

'Later that day, there was a knock on the door. It was the lad from the flat with the metal door. He said his friend was selling whizz – poor man's cocaine. Already drunk, I gave him money and he came in and shared the drug with me.'

'Laura …'

'I know. I wanted to fit in. I wanted to be everybody's friend. He was emaciated, a horrible person. He said I could have the carpet back which he had robbed out of the flat before I moved in. He had stripped the flat bare, copper, boiler, radiators. The council had replaced the necessary items, but not the carpet. He did the same thing when I moved out.'

I stopped writing and looked at Laura. She looked ashamed. 'I'm finding it hard telling you all this.'

'Shall we have a brew?' I suggested.

'Okay.' Laura walked to the kettle and switched it on to boil. She rolled a fresh cigarette and returned to the doorway to inhale its nicotine. She continued to impart information as smoke trailed from her mouth. 'His flat was a drug den. No electricity or gas. It was disgusting, a dive, cold and stark. He had a Staffordshire Bull Terrier. The dog was not fed, and he beat the poor animal.'

My pampered pooch was with me, Laura loves him. She looked out into the garden and watched my puppy frolic. 'I know it's disgusting.' Once again Laura and I sat facing each other, steaming mugs of liquid in front of us.

'I mean what I said. If you don't want to carry on, that's fine. I don't want you to be ill revisiting this dark time.' I offered.

'No, it needs to be said. The money would run out. I took my laptop to a Polish all-night shop. I got forty pounds for it. I thought I had excelled myself, I was disgusted with myself. I went back for the laptop and bought it for sixty pounds with money I had borrowed. It took me months to pay the money back because I was getting drunk all the time. Metal Door Guy, or his girlfriend, would knock on my door ten times a day. When the groceries you ordered were delivered, they would come around and "rinse me" of all my stuff. He offered me heroin to smoke, and I took it. I had to go shoplifting with him. I would be the distraction. I went because he threatened violence. He stole cider. The sort that has never seen an orchard, never mind an apple.' We both chuckled. I took a sip of my lukewarm drink.

'We were banned from shops. I had started to look and act like the company I was keeping. When he and his girlfriend robbed me, they took everything. Jewellery you had bought me. My laptop, handbags, everything, they left me with nothing.'

'I hated you living there.'

'I know, Mum. Once, when Dad came to see me, I was off my face. I just wanted him to go. I had taken a lot of crack the night before.'

'Poor Dad. I was so happy when you moved out.'

Laura found a place to rent – a bright, sunny upstairs flat with a bay window in a suburban area. Fully furnished, with a kitchen and shower room. The single bed was pushed against a wall in the living area. Laura sold her furniture and washing machine to a recovering alcoholic. He agreed on a price of £100 but he gave just £95 – for the furniture we had paid thousands for.

My cup of tea had now gone cold. 'Did you like the new place?'

'When I moved in, I was so relieved to be away from that flat, away from him and his girlfriend. I stopped drinking. I attended meetings. I got myself out and about. I went to the Alcohol Support Service centre for company. I felt safe. On my own, with a period of sobriety, my confidence grew. I thought I would be okay to start drinking, to moderate my intake. But, of course, my drinking shot out of control. I met a lad at the Support Centre and we shared crack and got wrecked together. After that it was just alcohol.'

This was the flat from which Laura was taken, half-dead, to a life-support machine.

Whizz/speed/amphetamine – cheap man's coke: My purpose is to energise and make you feel alert. I am proud to class myself as an 'upper'. I create excitement, encouraging your tongue to run away with itself. I can make you overactive, agitated or acutely psychotic. I accomplish false images, make you see and hear things that are not real. My high is followed by a long come-down. I love to make you irritable and depressed. Amphetamines were once the main ingredient of diet pills. You like this. You will not eat if I fill your needs. I will not allow you to relax or sleep, not when I am ready for action. As I become weak and begin to seep out of your body, you will feel miserable. I have the power to make this misery last for days. For sure, I will entice colds and flu to enter your body, because I have compromised your immune system.

Class B drug: Illegal to have, give away or sell. Speed prepared for injection becomes a Class-A drug. Possession: five years in jail, unlimited fine. Supplying: up to fourteen years and unlimited fine.

Smoking heroin, a.k.a. 'chasing the dragon': I have a huge following. Five years ago, global heroin users were estimated to be around fifteen to twenty-one million, aged between fifteen and sixty-four. This is how you smoke me: take a piece of tin foil and make a tube to inhale my vapour. With another piece of foil, create a flat surface. Place a chunk of me at one end of the foil, the one that is close to you. Apply gentle heat from a lighter to the under surface of the foil and heat me so I boil. Inhale my vapour deep into your lungs via the tin foil tube. Don't waste me. I have a need to get inside you, not disappear into the atmosphere. Some people have difficulty in chasing my vapour. I am strong and powerful, I completely overshadow you. This is why they call it chasing the dragon. Inhaling is safer than injecting, but much of me can be wasted. I yearn for more followers, so have made solo use difficult. I rush directly to your brain. I am a drug made from morphine, extracted from the opium poppy. I have been around for many thousands of years. Originally, I was used to treat pain, sleeplessness and diarrhoea. But that market was not as big as yours. My cousin, diamorphine, is stronger than me. He's greater than opium. He has been produced for medical use. My mate, street heroin, is sold as 'brown'. Sometimes clubbers will seek him out, for a chill after a big night out. A small dose of him creates a feeling of warmth and well-being. A bigger dose will make you sleepy and very relaxed. If you are new to using him, a first dose can cause dizziness and vomiting. He is highly addictive, he is proud of that. Invite him into your lungs, and he causes risk from inhaling vomit because he'll sedate and stop the cough reflex. Vomit stays in the airways so you cannot breathe. Ultimately, he has conquered you.

Through my research on drug use I found some more interesting information: Apparently, women tend to become dependent on drugs more quickly than men, and also find it harder to quit. However, women often take heroin in smaller doses, which may explain why more men die from overdoses than women.

3. New Depths

One Easter, Laura wanted to visit our home town to stay with a childhood friend. She assured me this friend did not drink alcohol.

The telephone rang, the day I was due to collect her for this Easter break. I got out of bed. 'Hi, Mum, can you come early. I'm ready. We could go for coffee.' I had a headache. Rob went to collect her. She insisted he take her to the supermarket. I opened the door to Laura, a bunch of flowers in her hand, she thrust them out to me. 'Happy Easter,' she said. She sat down on the hall rug and rummaged through her overstuffed bag. 'Here, take care of these.' She handed me the keys to her flat. I looked at them in wonder. I refused to take them. She stuffed the keys to the bottom of her bag. 'You know. Mum, I really have been quite ill, but I'm better now. I'm really happy.'

'That's good,' I said. Rob looked upward for a second, he gave a slight nod with his head. He brushed past us and left the house for work. 'What do you want to do? Go for coffee?'

'Nah, I'll go to my friend's house.' The friend, Tanya, who did not get out of bed before midday. 'Can you drive me, because my bag's heavy?' Off we went on the two-minute journey.

The next day, I sat in the passenger seat of Rob's van. He picked up speed, leaving the heavy traffic behind. His telephone rang, and connected to the hands-free device. 'Hi, it's Tanya.' My heart drove into my mouth. 'I don't mean to alarm you, but Laura is behaving oddly. She keeps walking into things. She thinks she has a brain tumour.'

'A brain tumour?'

'Don't worry. My partner and I will take her to A & E.' The call ended.

'What a load of bollocks … a brain tumour?' Rob said. I was silent, a wave of sickness overtook me.

That afternoon, Laura, Tanya and her partner stood at my door. More strangers I was forced to invite inside. 'It's not a brain tumour,' Laura said.

'Shall we have a brew?' Laura asked.

I switched the kettle on. 'I don't understand. What's wrong with you?' I asked.

'Nothing,' Laura said. 'Can I have a hug?' She walked toward me. I raised my hand, palm facing her. She went to the kitchen, where Rob was entertaining Tanya's partner. Tanya and I were alone in the room.

'I hope you don't think I took her out drinking last night.'

'No,' I lied.

'Laura was insistent on going to town, to the clubs. She said if I didn't go with her, she would go on her own. She said she wanted to find a husband.'

'A husband? She's a bloody crackpot!' What Laura wanted was someone to step in and mop up her mess.

'Don't tell Laura I told you.'

The entourage departed. Rob and I were flabbergasted.

The following Monday, I received a telephone call. 'Mum, I'm still unwell. Tanya is taking me to the doctor this evening.' Although our family doctor was no longer Laura's GP, he knew her, he cared.

'Ring me when you get back,' I said. Throughout the evening, I sat with the telephone in my hand. The phone I usually dreaded ringing was silent. At nine-thirty, I rang Laura's phone.

Tanya answered. 'I'll ring you back. Laura's just going to bed.'

'What the hell is going on?' I said to Rob.

'God knows.'

Tanya rang half an hour later. She said Laura may have bipolar. She added, 'It's treatable. It's just a case of finding the right medication.'

My poor daughter, my sick and vulnerable daughter, had a sickness. Something we could hang our coats on. No! We had been fed the bipolar story many times, only to be told, 'Nah, I've not got that.'

The next day, Laura called: 'Mum, can you come? I've taken all my medication. I've phoned for an ambulance.' I dropped the phone. I ran out of the house. Every limb of my body shook. I manoeuvred the car off the drive without thought. I headed, at speed, to Tanya's house. Laura ran out to greet me. Her face puffy, her eyes hidden behind slits.

'Oh, Laura …' I followed her into an empty house. 'What have you done?' Laura sat on a kitchen chair. I stood before her. 'Will you ever find happiness?' She did not look at me, she kept her attention on her hands she was wringing. 'What's put you in this state?'

Tanya walked in. 'Laura! I told you not to ring your mum.' Tanya looked at me. 'She hasn't taken her tablets. I have them. She's having an episode. It will pass.'

An episode? The ambulance crew arrived and the paramedics began speaking with Laura. It was clear they were familiar with her issues. Laura asked them if she could speak in private. So Tanya and I waited outside until we were allowed back inside.

'No need to take her to hospital,' the paramedic said. I cried at the repetition of it all. The crew threw looks of sorrow my way. They departed to attend to urgent matters.

'What are you playing at?' I asked Laura.

'I'm so unhappy.'

'Unhappy? You were at your happiest three days ago. Are you in debt?' Rob and I had paid arrears for her new flat on two separate occasions.

'No, she isn't,' Tanya said.

'If this is a stunt to force me to take you home, it's not working.' I went home. Dread dominated me. The telephone shrilled. I had to pick it up.

'I want to go back to my flat. Can you take me?' Laura asked.

'I am in no fit state to go anywhere. Get a taxi.' I was frightened by my own daughter. A slab of fear pressed on my chest.

'I've no money,' Laura said.

'Send the taxi to me before it picks you up. I will pay. Laura, make sure he comes here first. I don't want to see you.'

I watched out of the window for the taxi. I sat down. I could not relax in my own home. I was a tiny being with a mammoth problem. To ease myself, I stayed at the window. Somehow looking out at the world was easier than confining my eyes to my family home, where she used to belong. An hour passed. I watched people stroll by.

I picked up the sickening telephone. 'I've lost my keys to the flat. I can't go back.' The keys again, her ploy to stay.

'Ring your landlord. He'll have a spare key.' Half an hour later a taxi stopped at the bottom of my drive. The driver wanted paying.

That evening when Rob was home, the telephone rang. 'I'm back at my flat. Can you speak with my care worker?' Laura handed the phone over.

'Hi, Mrs Sefton, didn't you know Laura was in crisis? We thought it would be good for her to come home to you.' How could I know that! Who should have informed me? Where was the consideration for the parents? Did we not constantly cope with crisis? A horrendous situation to deal with when you are sober. Our daughter could escape through the doors of alcohol and drug seclusion. Yet she was the one who had support. She was the one whose needs were met.

All Laura's behaviour at Easter, in my opinion, was due to manipulation. She was in arrears with her rent. Rob and I paid it, again, but as always there was more to the tale than that.

When I questioned Laura, a little while back, about her drug use, I reminded her of this episode. 'I had been prescribed Antabuse to help with my craving for alcohol. I found that if I took a few I got a buzz from them. I took a handful that Easter, I had a psychotic episode. I was scared. God had come into my life. He told me I was going to find a husband and have a child.'

'What other drugs have you taken?' I asked.

'None. That's it. To be honest, drugs were not my thing. I took them when I was drunk. I never did drugs alone, apart from the Antabuse. Alcohol was always my preference to escape from feeling.'

I researched the new words Laura gave to me.

Antabuse: blocks an enzyme that is involved in metabolising alcohol intake, making people feel ill if they drink alcohol.

A psychotic episode: is an instance in which symptoms of psychosis – delusions, thoughts and beliefs unlikely to be true – are manifested. Hallucinations involve hearing, feeling, seeing, tasting or smelling things that are not there. The delusions and hallucinations almost always arise from a deeply depressed mood. Bipolar disorder: formerly known as manic depression, is a condition that affects a person's moods, causing them to swing from one extreme to another. Unlike simple mood swings, each extreme episode of bipolar disorder can last for weeks, and some people may seldom experience a 'normal' mood.

Wasted morphine

Rob telephoned me from work, 'Book me in at the doctor's. I've a terrible pain in my stomach.' The doctor prescribed anti-flatulence medication, but warned that if the pain didn't go away he should go to hospital emergency. That night, Rob ran a fever. He insisted he was fine and went to bed. When he awoke in the early hours, he asked me to take him to hospital. I was careful driving over the speed bumps in the road, to try and stabilise his dreadful pain.

At the hospital, Rob lay on a stark bed, in a cubicle. He lay in pain. A skinny nurse gave him an injection of morphine, a small dose. She looked at the remainder in the syringe. 'Let me know if you need more,' she said. He dozed and awoke to more pain. I pressed the buzzer for the nurse and asked for the remainder of the morphine. 'That's been wasted,' she said, thrown away. That was her explanation for the disappearance of the drug.

Rob had appendicitis and needed surgery to remove the appendix. I travelled home without him. After his operation, whilst he recovered in hospital, I collected Laura to visit her beloved dad. She looked well, and was smart in appearance.

Laura had worked at the hospital where Rob lay in bed. She sat by her dad's side and checked his notes. She looked at the wall above his bed. On a board, scribbled in felt tip pen, was a name above the term of team leader. 'I know her,' Laura said. 'We worked together on the wards, she mentored me as a student.'

'Just think where your career would be if you'd carried on working,' I said.

'I can get it back.' She looked out of the window to search the skyline, searching for where her career had flown.

Before Rob was due to come home from the hospital, a specialist visited him. I was in the room. It was a hot day. The window was open. 'Your appendix was enlarged and a lot of pus had oozed out of the sack. We will send it away for analysis.' The specialist looked over to me. I was standing by the window. 'Don't worry, he's a strong man.'

Rob was a strong and fit man. His work was physical, up and down ladders, lifting heavy machinery. He played squash to a high level. We took walks together. Our alcohol consumption was minimal and he did not smoke. Our diet was deliciously healthy. Of course, he would make a full recovery, and he did. Rob returned to work two weeks after his operation. Not recommended for his type of physical work, but in his mind the return was essential. He had customers to tend to, customers who might go elsewhere.

Laura did not telephone, she did not answer our calls. Rob and I were rendered stagnant with her antics. The telephone rang: Tanya. Rob answered. 'Laura is in a dreadful state, her flat is a mess, there are soiled clothes and excrement in her room, she is very down. I thought you should know.' That desperate feeling of utter sadness, that rush of anxiety, penetrated my soul. I craved to run and hide. Rob told Tanya not to call again.

Tenants from hell

The tenants now residing in the house we bought for Laura were a nightmare. The young couple we took pity on, the young couple we gave a chance to, terrorised the neighbourhood. I received numerous telephone calls relating to their behaviour. The old man who lived behind our house became most vocal. During one complaint, he added, 'I know your daughter. I know you as a parent. You will not give Laura money. I took her card to the cash machine to withdraw money for her.' I put the phone down. I knew about this old man, buying alcohol with my daughter's money, alcohol to share with him. Shame on him. Laura also employed taxi drivers to draw out cash and buy alcohol for her when she was not capable.

The Tenants from Hell kept several cats and a dog, in direct conflict with the tenancy agreement. Their animals fouled the neighbours' gardens. I told the young couple to get rid of their animals or they would be evicted. Swear words whizzed from the lad's mouth. He knew the law, he and his girlfriend. 'Get a court order,' he said.

Without our permission, the tenants had given refuge to a friend of his just out of prison. The ex-prisoner invited his girlfriend and child to share the compact house. The housing benefit agency paid the young couple's rent. In the hope of evicting them, I telephoned the agency and informed them our tenants were subletting. An inspector would visit to assess the situation. I heard nothing of this visit. I contacted the agency: a visit could not go ahead. The police advised against it, due to the violent nature of the residents. And to top it all, the benefits agency stopped payment to us because of the sublet. The gas and electric company contacted me regarding debts the young couple had accrued. 'Cut the supply off,' I said.

'No, we can't do that.'

The tenants sent me abusive text messages, threatening to trash our house they lived in. I went to the police station. A civil matter, the police officer said. I demanded to see a sergeant. He sent an officer to visit the tenants. The officer came to my house with a ripped piece of paper, the word sorry scrawled across the page. I employed a barrister to take the case to court. On the day of the hearing, I attended court. The tenants did not. They and their hangers on were ordered to evict. If they still resided after the given date, I could employ bailiffs. Under no circumstance were we allowed on our property before the date set by the court.

June 2013, three days before the set date of eviction, I was informed that the tenants had left. 'We're not allowed go in yet,' I said to Rob.

'Bollocks to that; it's my house.' We stood on the step of the abused property. Put the key in the door and entered. The escaped smell was nauseating. Months of trodden correspondence littered the carpets. Empty cans of energy drink lay in different directions. Dog foul or cat foul, I did not employ forensics, plastered the walls. The gas cooker had gone, the pipe sawn through. Upstairs was in a similar state.

A glass case with a broken spotlight was in the bedroom; equipment for growing marijuana. The worst of their depraved behaviour waited in the bathroom. The bath, half filled with brown water, had layers of human excrement stagnating there.

We hired a skip and set to work. I spent days clearing the mess in the house I was not allowed to be in. Everything was ripped out. Every wall and floor I scrubbed with bleach. It was exhausting. The due date for eviction came and went. Over the next two weeks, I painted every room and ceiling.

During this stressful time, Laura was riding several benders. I would return home from decorating, at night, to the answering machine stacked with messages from her. The phone continually rang. My mobile did the same. I pleaded with Laura to leave me alone. She knew about the destruction of our property. She knew I was busy renovating. I told her I was beyond exhaustion. I was frightened to be at home with the telephone; each time I put it down, it rang again. I had no choice. I changed my mobile and house number. Laura's only form of communication with me would be through the writing of letters.

At that same time, Rob had an appointment to visit hospital for a six-week check from his appendix operation. 'No, I'll go on my own. You carry on painting,' he said. Two hours later, my mobile sprang to life. I clambered down the ladders, a brush in my hand. A picture of Robs's handsome face lit the screen. I would not have expected a call from him. 'It's a tumour,' he said.

'What's a tumour?'

'In my appendix, they found a tumour.' I could hear the tremor in his voice.

'Wait there. I'll come and collect you.'

211

'No, I can drive home.'

I telephoned Rachael and told her the news. Rachael rang Laura.

Rob was booked into the hospital for a series of tests. A worrying time, during his busiest schedule. All tests came back negative. 'But,' the consultant said, 'I am going to pass your case file onto the cancer hospital for their opinion.' We came home and cracked open a bottle of champagne. I contacted Rachael, and withheld my number to Laura, to tell them the good news.

What fresh hell is this?

This chapter is the hardest to write, the hardest to have lived. Laura, please forgive me, you know how much I love you. I could not take any more. I was frightened by you. I had a deep sickness and dread of having to deal with you. I did not visit you when I was told you were dying; I did not visit you when you were transferred to a mental health unit. I am sorry.

Not long ago, I asked Laura to describe what happened that night we received the horrendous telephone call warning of our daughter's critical condition. I had, until now, not wanted to know. I had suffered enough. But this journey would not be complete without knowing the facts. What follows is from Laura's pen.

Laura: By this time I was drinking for oblivion, and my body was failing. Driven by fear, I habitually rang for ambulances. Concerned neighbours were doing the same. They would say, 'We heard a bang.' 'You weren't answering your telephone or door.' 'Your curtains have been closed for days.'

When an ambulance arrived, I would kick off. I told the paramedics that I was okay, told them to go away. Then I would scan the room for hidden bottles. I wanted to continue my bender.

My hair was a mess. Bedding and strewn clothes were soiled. Empty bottles, half-eaten plates of food. Food untouched was out of date. A pile of unopened letters that I could not bear to address. Sometimes I would not answer the door to the ambulance crew, but I knew they would telephone the police. This became a frequent occurrence. I was a regular at A & E.

I was embarrassed and ashamed, despite being drunk. I was dirty and unkempt. Neighbours became tired of my behaviour. They became distant from me. They told me I was disturbing their children. They told me to get help. I felt so alone.

This was standard behaviour: I would be admitted to hospital, I would escape. I'd order a taxi and stop at a cash point and go to an off-licence to buy booze. I would go back to my flat. Hospital staff would alert the police. Police would appear at my door and order another ambulance. And so I had a repeating pattern. On one such discharge, the police were asked to bring me back to the hospital because my pulse was abnormally high. I remember the police arriving at my door. If I did not go willingly they would arrest me. I was strapped to a stretcher because I was adamant I would not go with them. I struggled and caused wounds to my wrists. I became obsessed with the resulting scars. I had the wounds redressed because I had removed skin and caused further wounding.

I have no recollection of the time span, but my last memory, of course, was drinking in the flat. On 23 July 2013, I awoke, surrounded by people talking. I could hear machines whir, click and breathe. A bright light pierced the darkness of night.

I was told, 'Don't move. You are in hospital. We are taking the tubes out of your mouth so you can breathe for yourself.'

'Where am I? What's happened?' I heard my voice say.

'You have drunk yourself into a coma.'

I was frightened. I thought: Is this it? Am I going to die? I was told I was very poorly but stable. Later, I was informed a specialist hospital was on standby for consideration of a liver transplant. I recall this as the longest night of my life. Anxiety and fear enveloped me. Nurses performed their duties. I had various intravenous infusions attached. I was catheterised. I could not comprehend how this had happened without my recollection.

I was in intensive care. The unit was busy and loud throughout the night. The clock ticked slowly. I wondered how I would come back from this. I wondered if I would be better off dead. The nurse taking care of me said the on-call psychiatric team would visit me during the night. And they did. I was told I was to be admitted to a mental health ward for a few days, for monitoring and safety. I refused. They threatened to section me, so I complied.

I had not eaten for days. A nurse brought me a beef sandwich on white bread, quartered. She told me the sandwich was left over from tea-time. I ate it, I was ravenous. I asked the nurse for a mirror. I dreaded what my reflection would show. Was I wounded? I stared in the hand-held mirror. I looked rough, but not scarred. I had not washed for a long time. I felt vile. I had nearly died, yet my appearance meant everything to me.

The night staff handed over to the day shift on the intensive care ward. I was informed I would be transferred to the mental health ward shortly. An ambulance had been sent for. I was deemed medically stable. My liver was inflamed and some of my blood tests were abnormal. This could be managed by the medical team on the mental health unit. A few days in the mental health ward turned into four months.

My darling daughter suffered this alone. I was afraid to visit, afraid to comfort her. I could not let my mind be dragged into the depths she had pulled me down so many times before. I was in the process of burying previous heartache. I would not introduce a new one. Laura would spend this time alone in the hope that she would benefit from this incarceration, but it was stomach-wrenching for me to know that.

The mental health ward

I asked Laura to recount her stay on the mental health ward.

Laura: I arrived on the mental health ward via an ambulance with a nurse escort. They wheeled me in and I was met by a friendly care assistant. I felt sick, dizzy and disorientated. It was the end of July. The sun shone through the window from the world outside. My allocated nurse dressed me in a hospital gown. She gave me a blanket. On my feet were my own scruffy Ugg boots. My property was by my side in a hospital carrier bag: a pair of joggers and a dirty jumper, slashed down the middle. I assume it had been cut when the medics performed CPR on me in my flat.

I was wheeled into a side room. Here was a settee and an old stereo, there were board games. I flopped onto the settee. My nurse tried to perform a written assessment of me, she abandoned this, I was too ill to comply. I was taken to my room: a bed, a wardrobe and a set of drawers. I had nothing to unpack. I felt so unwell. I was allowed to sleep.

A doctor came into my room and woke me. He introduced himself and led me to the clinic. He took an in-depth medical history, reviewing the recent blood tests and ordering more. My liver was damaged. He asked where my bruises had come from. I did not know. I often had memory lapses, common for an alcoholic. He looked at the wounds on my wrists, the ones received by the handcuffed straps. He made no comment.

Some patients were allowed to leave the ward to attend appointments or to go into town. I was unable to leave the ward for the first two weeks. I was detoxing with the help of my old friend, Librium. I kept asking for more: that was my addiction. More alcohol, more pills, more of everything. The plan was for me to visit my flat with a member of staff to collect a few belongings. In the meantime, I had nothing. I was given a few clothes from the lost property box, t-shirts and leggings. I used toiletries provided in the ward, sachets that were rubbish. I had no makeup and hated this.

On the second day, I wanted to take a bath. I felt weak and asked for a carer to help me. Two care assistants came to my aid. One shampooed my hair with the content of a sachet. My hair did not feel clean. The other carer handed me a razor to shave my legs, the first time my legs had been shaved in weeks. I was obliged to hand the razor back, averting the chance to self-harm. One of the care assistants I came to dislike. I found her rude and abrupt. I felt that she looked at me with disgust.

The nurses and carers were casually dressed: jeans, t-shirts, Converse pumps. A chart was in use to register and monitor patients. At night, staff shone a large torch through a glass section at the top of the door. Sometimes this woke me.

I was about to be made homeless. In the chaos of my situation, other issues were more important to me. Clumps of hair had started to fall out of my head. I became obsessed with the notion of baldness. I was told I had alopecia. Every day, I asked the nurses to check my head for bald patches. I became acutely aware of a cigarette burn on my shoulder. I constantly asked staff and other patients if it looked a mess, if the scar would fade. I knew the answer to my questions. I am a nurse. I have come to understand that I was suffering with acute anxiety disorder and this manifested itself as OCD. I had begun repeating degrading ritualistic behaviours, by way of punishing myself for the harm I had done to myself and my family. I believed my dad would die if I did not carry out these acts. This was the lowest point of my life.

At mealtime, in a dining room, I sat at a round table with other patients. We went for a meal when we were summoned. Breakfast was optional. I chose cereal from the display and fresh orange juice. Lunch came at midday. I requested salad. Sometimes I got salad, other times not. Evening meal was served at five in the afternoon. I would ask for a yoghurt for dessert. Sometimes I would have fruit. Supper was optional at nine: pre-packed sandwiches, sachets of hot chocolate, or malt. I would ask for cereal. Sometimes I got cereal, other times not, my choices were no longer my own. We were supervised at mealtimes.

Bizarre behaviour surrounded me. I wrapped up in myself. A high dose of medication rendered me monotone. I remember a Spanish woman, pacing the floor, her hands held behind her back. And an old woman with dementia chain-smoked, she would knock on the door of the staff, repeatedly asking for cigarettes. She would turn the shower on and leave the taps running, then exit the bathroom and say, 'Has anyone got a cigarette?' She had long, matted hair worn in a ponytail. A nurse cut the treasured ponytail off.

One patient called himself Popeye. He would prod people with a stick. He carried a Bible and said he was God. Popeye became dirtier, smellier and cruder. He was always swearing. He would hide in the bushes, then jump out playing air guitar. He spat and dribbled, I avoided him.

A heroin addict, to her distress, had become overweight. She was in her twenties and covered in self-harm scars. She smashed a lightbulb and a bottle of aftershave to use the glass as a knife. If she was not first in any queue, she became agitated.

The mental health ward had its own culture, and I trusted the patients. I was one of them. Legal highs and weed were brought into the ward by patients who used the exit and entry facility. If found in possession, they would not be evicted. After all, where would they go?

When my own odd behaviour subsided, I was put in a room of four. A woman in her seventies rubbed her feet together at night, an annoying sound to others, but I found this noise comforting. To be in the presence of others and no longer alone.

I was not in contact with my family. Tanya, my friend since childhood, kept in touch throughout my troubles. With her partner, she visited me at the mental health ward. She shopped for me. She brought me toiletries and a gift of sweets. Tanya stayed for a while. I enjoyed her company. My best friend.

We were encouraged to take part in activities: painting, pottery, making cards. I would not join in, although I made a card once.

On hearing of Laura's experience, on reflection, I am proud of the fight my daughter put up, proud of the tenacity she had. While Laura was living this existence, I waited at home. I waited for a telephone call to tell me she had gone, to tell me she was dead. I would picture a crematorium. I wondered who would come to her funeral. I thought of music I should choose for the service, music she would like.

While Laura was incarcerated on the mental health ward, she did not know my telephone number. She no longer had access to Rob's mobile number, she had lost, or sold her phone which held the stored numbers. Due to Rob's ill health, the business number was transferred to Rachael's house. It was time for our son-in-law, Barry, to take charge. This telephone number had been in operation for over thirty years. We could not change it. Laura knew this number by heart, and began to ring constantly, she began to harass Rachael. Rachael telephoned the hospital and spoke to a member of staff, asked that Laura be denied the use of their office telephone. Laura used other patients' mobile phones, and continued to harass her sister and the business. Rachael purchased the 'choose to refuse' service from the telephone company, and began to block the numbers Laura telephoned from. Operation of the 'choose to refuse' could only be carried out and handled on a residential line. At that time, if the residential calls were diverted, and received to a mobile phone, the service could not be operated via the mobile phone. Rachael was at the hairdresser with me. Barry rang. He was extremely busy out on the road and felt unwell. Laura would not stop telephoning him, even though he told her to 'fuck off'. He returned home to use the residential line to ban the latest number Laura had obtained. This was a temporary measure. Laura was persuasive and found another person with a phone. Rachael contacted the police.

Our boys played in their garden the hot day the policeman arrived to talk with Rachael. She told the boys the police officer had come because Aunty Laura had been naughty. The officer told Rachael that Laura was well known to the police in the city where she lived. A colleague would visit and issue Laura with a warning. An officer visited Laura on the ward, and she was cautioned.

Rachael was bitter towards her sister, the tears she had shed for her, the devastation Laura had caused her parents. It took Rachael a long time to forgive and reconnect with her sister.

Time for Laura to be discharged from the mental health ward. She had nowhere to live so she was transferred to a supported housing complex. I received a letter from Laura that had a gentle cheerful tone. I snatched at courage, withheld my number and phoned her.

'Who's that?' she asked. Her voice was thick and dull.

'It's Mum.'

'It's who?'

'It's Mum, Laura, it's Mum.'

'Mum, I'm in hospital. I've taken an overdose. I've taken over a hundred co-codamol (paracetamol and codeine),' she drawled.

'Oh Laura, then I can't talk to you. I can't bear it.'

'Mum, please don't go. Talk to me. Mum, please stay.'

I put the phone down. I broke down and sobbed great wallops of sound. The phone rang, I answered to my sister. My crying would not stop. My elder sister was driving to my house, on her way to comfort me. I rang Rachael and told her the dreadful news. Rachael was by my side before my sister arrived. Rachael squeezed next to me on the stairs. Through my tears, I managed to say. 'I love her. I can't stop loving her.' I looked to Rachael, tears rolled down her cheeks.

Laura recovered. I knew this because no news came my way to the contrary.

She told me later she had hallucinated because of the overdose. She said, 'I thought I had blown it this time. I was sure I would die.'

Some time after this, we sat outside a restaurant in a shopping mall. The complex of restaurants gave the atmosphere of being on holiday. We each had a glass of Pepsi. We were waiting for our meal to be served. Two portions of a starter for Laura, a pizza for me.

'Did you want to die?' I asked.

'No, I never wanted to die.'

When she was discharged from hospital, her belongings were at the establishment she had taken the overdose at. She was not allowed to go back, because she had abused medication and broken the rules.

Laura's care worker, along with Laura, had a meeting with Laura's ex-landlord. He was persuaded to relet the flat to Laura.

Rob would telephone his daughter during this period to reach out to her, but he always withheld his number. Sometimes, Laura would write me a letter. My hand shook when I saw her handwriting on the envelope.

Gaining perspective

An appointment for Rob to attend the cancer hospital landed on the mat. 'Don't worry,' I said. 'They're just making sure you haven't got cancer.'

We arrived at the hospital on the given day. The waiting room heaved with sick people and their care-worn relatives. Two hours passed sitting on the uncomfortable chairs. 'Let's go home,' Rob said. He wanted to get back to work. Then his name was called and we were ushered into a small room with a bed, two chairs and a sink.

The consultant arrived with his registrar. They sat on the edge of the bed and we sat on the chairs. The consultant began to draw a diagram. Rob's face grew pale. Intestines and lungs were sketched onto paper. The specialist began to explain his diagram. 'The type of tumour you had in your appendix is extremely rare, affecting only 0.04 per cent of the population. Cancers of the appendix usually spread to the abdomen in the majority of patients. I'll have to inspect your intestines with the aid of a camera. Seeds from the tumour may have planted in the belly button, so I'll whip that away …'

I looked at Rob. He was leaning to one side.

'Can I stop you, please?' I said. 'I think my husband is going to faint. Can he lie down?'

Both medics stood. Rob was apologetic.

'Don't worry,' the consultant said. 'It's usually the fit ones that keel over. Shall I come back?'

'No, carry on,' Rob said.

The consultant smiled, a sad smile. 'While screening, I will remove anything suspicious. I may remove part of your bowel at the site of the appendix. When you are under anaesthetic, you will receive a treatment called hyperthermic intraperitoneal chemotherapy, HIPEC for short. This chemotherapy is heated to forty-five degrees and left in your abdomen for ninety minutes. All in all, the operation should take about twelve hours.'

'What's the alternative?' I asked. Rob had lost the desire to communicate, both his hands were clamped to his forehead.

'If left to chance, you will very likely be back here in five years, and I will be telling you the result is inoperable.' The consultant looked at Rob.

'There is no choice,' I said. 'It's procedural. You have to have it done.' I returned my attention to the man who held my husband's future in his hands. 'We have a holiday booked in two weeks. Will it be okay to go?'

'My advice? The sooner you get the procedure done the better.' The holiday was cancelled.

Rob was sent for blood tests. He visited the stoma nurse, in case a stoma should need fitting. As Rob lay on the bed, his arms across his chest, the nurse marked the spot with a pen where the stoma should be sited. She covered the markings with gauze to preserve the pen marks. Rob and I left the hospital, like dead men walking.

We travelled to Rachael's house. Explained the diagnosis. 'Don't tell Laura,' I said. Laura would make this drama her own. I wanted to devote my emotions to Rob. I could not cope with her. And we were all but estranged from Laura. It would be cruel for her to be alone in her concern for her beloved dad.

Rob dreaded having a stoma fitted, a bag to collect excrement. 'It won't change our lives,' I said. 'I'll make sure of that.' During his operation, a section of bowel had been removed. The consultant rang me when the operation was complete. 'Has he got a stoma fitted?' I asked.

'No, I know this was a concern of his.'

'He'll be so pleased.' I drove to the hospital. I waited in a room closed off to the intensive care ward. A machine on the wall delivered a free plastic apron. I tied it around my waist. I sanitised my hands. I waited to be invited in. I walked towards Rob's bed in the dimly lit room. Tubes crossed his body like angel's hair. A nurse sat at a computer by Rob's side. She studied each monitor reading connected to his body. I took hold of his hand. His face was swollen, his eyes were just slits.

'Why have you come?' He croaked.

'To see you.'

'I don't want you here. You're upsetting me,' he murmured. I knew what he meant. He did not want to upset me, seeing him like this. I kissed his damp forehead and went home.

I spent each afternoon and evening by Rob's bedside. I felt sorry for the patients who had no visitors. What was their story? What was their family background? And yet I did not find the strength to visit my own daughter when she had been in hospital. How lonely she must have been. I ate meals in the cafeteria. Rob recovered quickly, his level of fitness a contributing factor.

On 5 November 2013, Rob could come home. A dark day, where fireworks lit the sky. I arrived at the hospital to collect him. He sat in the day room, frustrated at having to wait for a consultation before coming home. He complained of not feeling well and returned to his bed to lie down. The registrar appeared. 'Good news, you can go home.'

'My husband's not feeling well,' I said. Rob sat quietly in his discomfort, he was desperate to come home. The registrar moved to the bedside. Rob complained of pain in his chest and a tightening of his left arm. He writhed on the bed. Sweat poured from him, his face a contortion of panic. The registrar pushed a red button on the wall. Staff came running. Rob was injected. A spray rushed under his tongue. I stroked his forehead, pleaded with him to be calm. *Please don't leave me.* Plastic circles with a metal nipple were attached to various parts of his body and linked to a machine to record his heart rate. An ECG was performed. The registrar said the reading was not showing a heart attack. Maybe Rob had a blood clot. More doctors and nurses surrounded the bed. After the intervention, Rob became calm and fell asleep.

To determine if a heart attack had taken place, a blood sample was taken at the time of the pain. A second blood sample would be drawn twelve hours later, for comparison.

Rob was comfortable and in capable hands. I kissed his hot forehead, listened to his deep breathing. I drove home to loud bangs and sprays of light. I opened the front door and went to bed, my mobile telephone held tightly in my hand. Early next morning, Rob rang. 'I've had a heart attack.'

'Have you?'

'The blood test came back positive for a heart attack.'

'How are you feeling?'

'Well, it's not good, is it?'

'You'll be fine. They'll sort you out at the hospital. Imagine, ten minutes later and you would have been on the motorway with me yesterday.'

A pioneering hospital in close proximity to the cancer hospital catered for heart patients. Rob's condition was considered critical. He waited at the cancer hospital until a bed at the cardiac hospital became available. Paramedics would transport him. He could not come home.

When he was bedded down in the cardiac hospital, a problem arose. The fitting of a stent to unblock Rob's artery was the preferred procedure. But Rob is allergic to aspirin, and aspirin is used in the aftercare of a stent fitting. The alternative procedure was a heart bypass. The operation was carried out. Rob was placed in intensive care before returning to the ward. In total, Rob had been in hospital for six weeks.

I share these events to show how I gained perspective. For twelve years I had been consumed by the fear of my daughter's health. Concentrating on Laura, this had happened to Rob, the pearl of my existence. I had a lot to be grateful for, a lot to look forward to. A life to live for myself and to share with Rob.

Laura was still unaware of her dad's health situation.

Christmas was on its way. Time to visit Laura and bring her home for Christmas Day. Rob was much recovered and looked in good health. We entered Laura's flat. I sat on the bed in the small room and asked Laura to join me. I took her hand in mine. 'I have something to tell you,' I said. I explained Rob's illness.

She cried. 'I'm a shit for not being there for Dad. I'm so sorry.' She looked at Rob. 'Are you all right now? Dad, promise you are?' Laura felt tremendous guilt for not being there for her dad.

'I'm fine. I'll be having regular checks. I'm fine.'

Laura dried her tears.

'Were you okay on the mental health ward?' I asked, still feeling guilty for not visiting her.

'Horrendous, I never want to go there again.' Laura finished packing her bag for home. We filed out of her flat as if nothing had been discussed.

In January, I telephoned Laura and withheld my number. 'Hi, how's it going?'

'Can you ring me back this evening?' she asked.

We did as we were bid. Rob rang her in the evening. 'Dad,' she said, 'I'm £700 in arrears for my rent.'

'I'm not bailing you out this time.' End of conservation. Laura was evicted.

She found refuge in a supported accommodation facility where staff made regular checks for alcohol and substance abuse. This facility was not as strict as the rehabilitation centre.

4. Victory

To escape the turmoil I was going through, I enrolled on a course: Write a Novel. I began to type, to change focus. I was able to process my emotions through the written word. I completed a first draft. Before I reworked my manuscript to be the best it could be, I needed to develop a writer's platform to enable the selling of my work. For this, I decided to write a blog. But what could I blog about? Writing? No, I was new to the game. Bloggers of writing had too much experience for me to compete. But I did have a story to tell: a mother's journey alongside her alcoholic daughter.

I had spent years suffering in silence, in a way that no other person, who has not had their child ripped from them by addiction, will truly understand. I deliberated. Was I capable of revisiting the pain of my daughter's addiction? Each time I recalled a memory I felt sick. But I was convinced. I had to do it. I wrote to Laura and asked permission to chart her life. Selflessly, she agreed.

I researched the ways of blogging. I enrolled on a course to make my blog professional. I began to type the chapters of my daughter's life, and my life alongside her. I honed and edited each snippet. When I reached a handful of posts I began to blog. I opened my door, and my heart, to the public. Rachael posted a link to my blog on Facebook. The first day of airing, my blog attracted over 1,400 views. In accordance with the course advice, I posted short pieces, with humour and tears. Laura's popularity rose in tune with the blog. Friends old and new contacted her, many of them not realising how she had been struggling in life. At this time, Laura was in sheltered accommodation. Staff and other inhabitants read the blog. They were interested, but mainly saddened, by its content. They could relate to the destruction her behaviour had caused her loved ones. I was in contact with Laura, she read the blog daily as I posted, and that's where the miracle happened – she saw how loved she was and decided to recoil from drinking alcohol. It was a turning point. My blog saved my daughter's life.

Rachael phoned one evening, saying her friend thought I should not blog about Laura's life because it made for uncomfortable reading. Rachael pulled the link from her Facebook page. I continued to blog. The life of an alcoholic makes for uncomfortable living, yes, but I had to blog honestly. The mother of an alcoholic has no brushes or filters to highlight the journey she is forced to take. The reason I blogged heartache, why I let the secrets of my family be known? There are a lot of addicts out there suffering in silence. Their lives are wrecked. If they are brave enough, strong enough, they seek help. They share their addiction mayhem, their chaotic lives. They try to make sense by relating to other addicts. For every one addict captured by abuse, several loved ones are left in their wake, grieving and agonising. I wanted to show my daughter was, and is, a vital human being, not a sad drunk easily dismissed from life. I wanted to show the risk of losing one's way. People suffering the same horrendous journey as ours could gain some perspective by hearing our story.

That, at least, was my intention, but things were to take a surprising turn. One night I was in the kitchen with my two grandsons, lifting freshly baked cookies off the tray while making sure the boys did not burn their hands. There was a knock at the door, and Rob answered it. Two policemen stood there and asked if they could have a word with 'Mrs Sefton'.

'What for?' asked Rob.

'It's regarding her blog.'

Rob invited the policemen into the family room and I herded the boys to the sitting room, a cookie in each hand. 'Don't worry about the police. I'll explain in a minute,' I said to the boys.

'Do they want a cookie?' my youngest grandson asked.

I joined Rob and the officers in the family room. Rob showered me with his sternest look. He didn't like the fact that I was writing a blog and exposing our family troubles to the world. Now it looked like it was about to bring more trouble.

James had reared his ugly head. His current girlfriend was receiving malicious mail. In these letters, my blog was mentioned.

'So what are you saying?' Rob asked. 'Do you think Laura is sending the letters?'

'We're following a line of enquiry at this stage.'

'It's not Laura's style,' I said. Laura would demand immediate gratification, she would be more likely to harass by telephone. She would thrive on the drama of a face-to-face slanging match. She would not be inclined to buy paper, envelope or stamps. She would not go to another city to post a letter, as the postmark on the envelope stated. I was not trying to hide my daughter. I knew it was not her doing. 'Can you show me the handwriting?' The envelope passed to me showed none of the characteristics of Laura's handwriting. To clarify, I presented the officers with a piece of her penmanship. They were satisfied and left.

Rob looked at me. A look I could read: See what you've done. Brought more shit to our door. With regret, I agreed.

Despite the blog's growing popularity (with more than 50,000 worldwide views at last count), I decided to suspend it.

Soup kitchen

Laura was making progress in the supported house. As a reward, she was given a flat of her own on the complex. I was back in frequent contact with her. It was the time my blog was most popular. She asked Rob and me to visit.

I put the postcode in the sat-nav. I took deep breaths throughout the journey. Rob was quiet. We arrived on the street, pleasantly surprised to find newly built and gated apartments. We were not sure which was hers, so I phoned and she came to greet us. She looked tired and my heart swam down. But as we climbed the metal steps to her 'penthouse' apartment, and took our coats off, she relaxed. Laura had been awake all night. She had a headache from the excitement of our visit. As we relaxed over coffee, so did her face. We filed down the metal steps to wave goodbye. We hugged. Rob had tears in his eyes.

I began to visit Laura regularly. I took her shopping for food, treats, her favourites. I took her shopping for clothes.

Laura had a regulatory pin number for nursing, allowing her to practice. The 'pin' is reissued yearly, at a fee. I had paid the fee in the past. I had not wanted her to let go of her pin number, her career. If a nurse has not worked for three years, the pin cannot be reissued. As this was the case for Laura, she applied for a course to refresh her skills and to reinstate her pin number. She was excited by the prospect of returning to nursing. She was proud of herself as a nurse. She felt it in her bones: she would be accepted on the course. I quivered in my bones that she would not.

During one of my visits to the sheltered accommodation, Laura asked if I would meet the staff. They were reading my blog. Laura and I walked into the main building that housed patients. A young man came out of a room. He said hi to Laura. He looked at me coyly. 'This is Ricky,' Laura said.

As my visits to Laura multiplied, I saw signs of a connection between Laura and Ricky. 'Are you seeing Ricky?' I asked.

'No, we're friends. He cooks for me, he's a chef. We eat meals together.'

Ricky, a recovering alcoholic, began voluntary work at a soup kitchen, using his cooking skills to feed the homeless. He encouraged Laura to help prepare food and serve meals. I asked her to describe the soup kitchen.

Laura: The building was on the corner of a busy street in town. Traffic hurtled past, unaware of the significance of this brightly coloured construction. The building wraps around the corner, like the arms of the owners wrap around the vulnerable. The large windows, sectioned into squares, welcome visitors.

I was in the company of Ricky and another man, both of them had helped at the soup kitchen before. Ricky had the keys to enter the building. There were two locks to open. Ricky locked the door behind us. The area outside was littered with drunks, with drug users. We recognised the look on their faces, the way they dressed, the way they carried themselves. We knew some of them.

We entered a large room that smelt damp and musty. In this room were large tables, various donated chairs pushed neatly underneath. I looked at the walls. Pictures there were held by drawing pins. The pictures, cut and stuck, were a colourful reference to God, love and peace. I noticed a donation box. I picked it up and shook it: empty. I had been advised not to take my mobile phone, cash card, or anything of value. I was aware of this, I know how the desperate mind works.

I followed Ricky to the compact kitchen, which was in need of a clean, and structural work. The appliances were rusty. We had visited the kitchen the day before to check what had been left by Fair Share, the charity which collects donated food from supermarkets to deliver to the needy. Ricky wanted to know what ingredients he had to work with. He took sausages, mince meat and liver out of the freezer to defrost. The next day, we bought onions to make gravy. Ricky was in charge. He switched on the ovens, collected large pans and prepared a stew. I peeled huge amounts of carrots, potatoes and onions. Good tears fell from my eyes, forced out by the innocent vapour of onion.

We had arrived at the building at three-thirty. The doors would open to the helpless and hungry at six-thirty. The kitchen soon became hot. We prepared food and washed pots. I moved out of the kitchen into the cool large room. I set the tables with knives and forks. I stood back to admire the banquet setting.

At five o'clock the doorbell chimed. Ricky walked to the door to check who had pressed the button. He recognised the elderly woman and allowed her access. My eyes were drawn to the gold cross worn around her neck. She was a big woman, well fed. She surveyed the room. She assessed me. She told me I had arranged the tables wrongly. To avoid upset, I rearranged to her specification. 'And put napkins out,' she shouted across the room. The napkins she referred to? Paper towels. 'And the jugs of juice should be placed on the tables.' The liquid refreshment waited in the fridge, chilling. 'We must treat people like the Queen, regardless of who they are.'

Though I took a dislike to this woman, I agreed with her sentiment. In time I grew to like and respect her. She was a former surgical nurse.

Six o'clock arrived. The food was almost ready. Wholesome smells bathed the room. The door bell rang. The woman with the gold cross on her ample bosom became vocal. 'They can wait outside. It's not six-thirty and it's not raining.'

Ricky had organised macaroni cheese to offer to the Muslim guests.

I watched the gold-cross woman open the door. The winter air rushed in before the destitute. I stood with other helpers at the head of the table. Ricky was in the kitchen. The queue of the hungry was not orderly; people rushed forward and asked for soup to be ladled into the bowls, they came for second helpings.

These individuals shared the same appearance: frayed clothes, jogging bottoms and jeans, all of the clothes in need of laundering. There were more men than women.

A woman wearing bright makeup attracted my attention. I could smell sweet scent from her with no depth to it. I complimented her. She told me she 'shopped' at Boots, the chemist. Her oral hygiene was poor, some teeth were missing. She handed me empty ice-cream tubs and asked me to fill them with food. Her partner was unwell, had tried to kill himself. I fulfilled her request. She asked for a carton of orange juice. I went to the kitchen and fetched two. I was not supposed to supply takeaway food or drink, but I wanted to help. I knew what it was to be in need.

Ricky had been preparing meals at the soup kitchen for weeks before my first visit. He told me he was worried about an anorexic prostitute who was absent that night, we did not find out why she kept away.

We began to serve the main course. Everyone got up from their empty soup bowls. They took a plate from a pile. They jostled for serving. Most people wanted everything: pile my plate high. One man appeared drunk. I offered to carry his plate to the table. He declined.

I served a man I recognised, a previous occupant at the facility where I live. We used to get along. He was barely recognisable. He wore a dirty overcoat and jeans with holes in. He carried a full beard, not the clean-shaven face I knew him by. He had arrived with another man in the same condition as him. He told me he was drinking and using crack cocaine. He wanted me to ask the facility where I live if he could return. He wanted help. His friend was blind in one eye and had mouth cancer. They ate their meal and stood to leave. I rushed over to the man I knew for his telephone number. I would contact him regarding the facility. He did not have a number. I guessed he sold his mobile phone.

The homeless, hungry lined up for second and third portions. For some, it was their only meal of the week.

People thanked us for the delicious food. They opened the door and stepped onto the busy street. Walked into the cruel night air.

I helped with the pot washing. Grateful, proud and blessed that I was serving and not receiving.

Anglesey

I invited Laura to spend a weekend with Rob and me on the coast, a reward for her continuing improvement. We set off in our car, all three of us. Laura sat in the back. As we approached the first sighting of the coast, I said, 'Look, Laura, you've not seen the sea for a long time.'

'No, and it's lovely.' She was pleased with her recovery. Happy to enjoy things that alcohol had placed a veil over.

We arrived at the lodge we were to stay in. Bags unpacked, we sat outside on the decking overlooking the sea. It was a bright sunny day. 'Do you mind if I have a cigarette, or would you rather I go somewhere else to smoke?' She asked.

'No, Darling, you have your cigarette here with us,' said Rob. It had been a long time since Rob had called his daughter 'Darling'. Laura rolled a cigarette. I gave her a saucer for the ash.

Early evening, before dinner, Rob asked, 'Is it okay Laura if I have a glass of wine?'

'Dad, it's fine to drink in my company. If you don't have a glass of wine you won't want me to come again. Anyway, it's not the sort of drinking that affects me. I wouldn't be happy in the company of someone drinking to excess, it's that sort of behaviour I am at risk of. You have your drink and chill out.'

I poured Rob a glass of cold white wine. I hoped Laura was not listening to the glug-glug of the liquid falling into the glass. I grabbed myself a bottle of beer and flipped the lid off. I had bought Laura a selection of fruit juices and fizzy drinks. We sat around the table, breathing the sea air and listening to the seagulls, with my daughter by my side.

The next day, we walked along the beach. I could enjoy the sound of the gulls, the rushing of the sea, the soft texture of sand under my feet, the squeals of delight from children. I was no longer in that dark place where these things hurt me and reminded me of the loss of my daughter. 'Mum, why don't you carry on with the blog and finish it? It's helped a lot of people.'

'Dad's not keen for me to do it. And anyway, I have done that now.'

Laura bent down and picked up a perfect shell. Carefully she placed it in her pocket. When she was a girl, I used to call her a beachcomber. She loved to inspect the tiny details of nature's gifts. 'I have been toying with the idea of expanding the blog and writing a book.'

'You must, Mum.'

'You know Laura, I think the blog helped save your life. You found perspective through reading about your life. Realising how much you are loved. You were able to see how your hideous situation affected us all.' That is the isolation of addiction. The only voice she heard had been her own.

'I know. Write a book. Promise you will. Let some good come out of this.'

'Maybe I will.'

'No, Mum, shake on it.' She held out her hand and I placed mine in hers. 'It's a deal. You have to do it now.'

We packed our belongings and prepared for the journey home. 'I'll have to find a place to live soon. If you have anything I can have? Knives and forks, that sort of thing.'

My daughter had nothing. Yet she had everything: a future to look forward to.

Reflections

Laura and I realised we needed to share our reflection on her alcoholism and my journey through that.

Laura: My drinking was fun, then it became fun with a problem, which turned into a huge problem.

My active alcoholic years were a mixture of chaos and oblivion. I sought out and courted both. I learnt through the twelve-step programme/support groups that I had an 'alcoholic head'. A crazy head which never seemed to slow down without the aid of alcohol or drugs.

I struggled and found it hard to cope with everyday living. A luxury that I thought others took for granted. I always wanted to know what was next. I became bored easily. I remember feeling this way from an early age. I wanted to feel different. I wanted to look different. I wanted to be different.

I find it hard to catalogue events during the drinking years. Maybe this is nature's way of protecting me from unwanted memories. I am aware my family was not awarded this luxury.

My drinking damaged me; stunted my emotional growth. It was supposed to ease my pain but it caused me even more pain.

I believed being an alcoholic was my identity: 'I can't help it, I'm an alcoholic ... I behave this way because I'm an alcoholic.' I embraced the role of the victim, which inevitably fuelled more drinking.

I did love alcohol, but the love affair ended. Years of heartache got me to where I am now. The person I am today. The only cure for alcoholism, in my opinion, is complete abstinence. Believe me when I say I tried everything not to drink. I see now that drinking was a grieving process, first anger and loss, then sadness. I missed and craved my old existence of being an alcoholic, bizarre as that sounds, but alcoholism was my normality. Through the bottle I could escape into oblivion.

I was born into a supportive loving family and was encouraged to fulfil my dreams, but this did not stop me drinking. I saw my parents' role as rescuers when drinking was unbearable, then as enablers when I wanted to borrow money or be bailed out. My role was that of a manipulator, a role in which I was an expert, and I bore little guilt. Alcohol yielded power over me. I did not always want to stop drinking. I wanted to drink without consequence.

Could I have stopped drinking when I had a choice? Did I have a choice? The answer is that I do not know.

Do I believe alcoholism is a disease, genetics, or a choice? I do not know. I choose to leave that debating society of fear for drinking again. If I have a disease will I ever get well? Am I well? Today I choose to be sober.

If I had my time again with Laura as a child, a teenager, a young woman, I would do things differently. I would have cut her adrift sooner and let her float away in the hope she would throw down an anchor. We did too much for her, financially and emotionally. It had all been fruitless in changing her path. You cannot change the way a person behaves. The only power you have is to change the way you react to their behaviour. You cannot keep giving love unconditionally. The addict has to give something back. They have to earn love and respect, relearn to love themselves. A person who supports an addict is not in a relationship with them, they are in a codependent mess.

Love in a hopeless place

'Mum, I've started a relationship with Ricky,' Laura said through the telephone. I was pleased. A good man with a shared history of abuse. Some may think this a bad thing, and that they may encourage addictive behaviour in each other. Share a bottle of vodka. But I see they support each other.

They understand the pitfalls and know what to avoid. They have a shared pain. They have the connection both have searched for.

Time for Laura to move out of the sheltered facility. There was a waiting list for a place such as that. A flat was offered to her by the authorities. A flat she had no choice but to take.

An upstairs flat on a cul-de-sac. No carpet to caress underfoot. No furniture to sit and rest on. Refuse bins were tipped over in the street. Empty cans of cider rolled in the wind. Painted numbers in huge white lettering on the brick walls differentiated each flat. It is an area where drunks and drug users, society's unwanted, live. This was where my darling girl was placed.

Ricky would not allow Laura to live there alone. He left the facility before his allotted time to move in with her. To care for and protect her. Laura and Ricky went to a charity shop for the homeless and chose two chairs and a coffee table. Ricky's parents bought them a bed. His nana paid for a roll of carpet. Rob and I bought the white goods for the kitchen. Rachael and Barry gave money for bedding.

There was a lot of anti-social behaviour in this close. People knocked on Laura's door to ask if Laura and Ricky wanted to share drugs. They had the strength to say no, they had each other.

Although I was unhappy with Laura's living conditions, I was not distraught. I saw in Ricky a man who would protect and look after her. She was no longer lonely.

The day arrived for Laura to be interviewed for the return to nursing course. So far, she had a one hundred percent pass rate at interview. She had noted her history of abuse on the application form. Laura was asked about current legislation regarding the role of a nurse. She did not know the answer, being out of the loop for so long. Would the course not have taught her that? She was not accepted to update her pin number, and was advised to go away to research articles. I worried this failure would hit her hard. I was wrong.

As you know, I wanted Laura to have a successful career. Now this is of little importance to me. I yearn for her to be happy and well.

I arrived at the gruesome flat to take Laura shopping. 'I've been awake all night,' she said. 'The couple underneath are always fighting. I rang the police. Then a dog ran out and was savaged by another dog. That poor dog, the sound of pain it made.' I climbed the uncarpeted stairs and followed Laura into the room overlooking the horrible close. Ricky sat by the coffee table, preparing roll ups.

'You need to get on to the housing department. Go to Citizens Advice. I think you are at risk of failing if you stay here. Explain this to them.' Many visits and phone calls later, Laura and Ricky were offered a two-bedroom house with a garden and shed. A new house, on a new development. We were all thrilled. A house that would become a home. Ricky stood in the garden and cried the day the keys were handed over. 'Bliss,' Laura said, 'to have my own garden to sit in.' I relayed this message to Rob. The tears in his eyes were allowed to fall.

I asked Laura if her liver had recovered. 'Yes, it has. I'm very lucky.' Indeed she is. The liver is a filter for blood. It is a factory performing over five hundred chemical interactions in the body. Laura had narrowly avoided getting cirrhosis, an untreatable scarring which results in unrepairable damage of this vital organ.

Four years on, Laura and Ricky are still a couple supporting one another. He adores and cares for her. She thrives on his commitment. Ricky is part of our family, and Laura is a part of his.

I have found peace through my daughter's recovery.

If she chooses to abuse again, I will be desperately sad. But I am now able to move on with my feelings and place dread behind me. I will not wander the dark and lonely lanes my mind once weaved through.

My daughter was hurting and she made a terrible choice in how to ease that pain. Today, her choice is to be sober, to be happy and well. I love Laura when she is being Laura.

The name Laura is the feminised form of Laurus, Latin for bay laurel plant, which in the Greco-Roman era was used as a symbol of victory, honour or fame. Laura has earned the right to her name. She is victorious over alcoholism and drug abuse. She has restored honour to her family. Who knows, she may be famous, one day.

– The end –

REFERENCES

Crandell, Todd. (2013) There's more than one way to get to Cleveland. Ohio: Racing for Recovery

Alcohol Concern: https://www.alcoholconcern.org.uk

ABOUT THE AUTHOR

Lesley Sefton is not just the mother of a recovering alcoholic, drug abuser – she is also a business woman and a high achiever. She has two daughters, two grandsons, and a dog named Dexter. Lesley loves walking, reading, travelling abroad and her favourite pastime – writing.

Connect with her at: www.lesleysefton.com

23162673R00148

Printed in Poland
by Amazon Fulfillment
Poland Sp. z o.o., Wrocław